AF695302

METHODOLOGICAL FRAMEWORK FOR UNLOCKING MARITIME INSIGHTS USING AUTOMATIC IDENTIFICATION SYSTEM DATA

A Special Supplement of *Key Indicators for Asia and the Pacific 2023*

OCTOBER 2023

ASIAN DEVELOPMENT BANK

ADB

Creative Commons Attribution 3.0 IGO license (CC BY 3.0 IGO)

© 2023 Asian Development Bank
6 ADB Avenue, Mandaluyong City, 1550 Metro Manila, Philippines
Tel +63 2 8632 4444; Fax +63 2 8636 2444
www.adb.org

Some rights reserved. Published in 2023.

ISBN 978-92-9270-366-0 (print); 978-92-9270-367-7 (electronic); 978-92-9270-368-4 (ebook)
Publication Stock No. FLS230401-2
DOI: http://dx.doi.org/10.22617/FLS230401-2

The views expressed in this publication are those of the authors and do not necessarily reflect the views and policies of the Asian Development Bank (ADB) or its Board of Governors or the governments they represent.

ADB does not guarantee the accuracy of the data included in this publication and accepts no responsibility for any consequence of their use. The mention of specific companies or products of manufacturers does not imply that they are endorsed or recommended by ADB in preference to others of a similar nature that are not mentioned.

By making any designation of or reference to a particular territory or geographic area, or by using the term "country" in this publication, ADB does not intend to make any judgments as to the legal or other status of any territory or area.

This publication is available under the Creative Commons Attribution 3.0 IGO license (CC BY 3.0 IGO) https://creativecommons.org/licenses/by/3.0/igo/. By using the content of this publication, you agree to be bound by the terms of this license. For attribution, translations, adaptations, and permissions, please read the provisions and terms of use at https://www.adb.org/terms-use#openaccess.

This CC license does not apply to non-ADB copyright materials in this publication. If the material is attributed to another source, please contact the copyright owner or publisher of that source for permission to reproduce it. ADB cannot be held liable for any claims that arise as a result of your use of the material.

Please contact pubsmarketing@adb.org if you have questions or comments with respect to content, or if you wish to obtain copyright permission for your intended use that does not fall within these terms, or for permission to use the ADB logo.

Corrigenda to ADB publications may be found at http://www.adb.org/publications/corrigenda.

Notes:
In this publication, "$" refers to United States dollars.
ADB recognizes "China" as the People's Republic of China and "Russia" as the Russian Federation.

Cover design by Eric Suan.

On the cover: Ships from an ADB-funded Domestic Maritime Transport Project at Malé's domestic harbor (Malé North Harbor), the central hub for the distribution of goods in Maldives (photo by Ariel Javellana).

Contents

Tables, Figures, Boxes, and Python Scripts

Tables

Figures

Boxes

Python Scripts

Foreword

The advent of big data has significantly supplemented official statistics by addressing the lack of timely information. Official statistics traditionally rely on surveys, censuses, and administrative data, which often involve time-consuming data collection, processing, and analysis. This process leads to delays in obtaining relevant information which limits the ability of different stakeholders to make real-time decisions or respond promptly to emerging trends. Big data refers to the massive volume, velocity, and variety of data generated from various digital sources, such as social media, sensors, online transactions, and mobile devices. One emerging source of big data is the Automatic Identification System (AIS), a traffic navigation system originally designed to prevent vessel collisions during navigation. AIS messages transmitted by vessels worldwide constitute big data because of their high volume, velocity, and variety of information. The real-time availability of AIS data has sparked growing interest among researchers in the potential of using such data to generate real-time indicators of maritime shipping and trade. This special supplement to the *Key Indicators for Asia and the Pacific 2023* delves into the capacity of AIS to provide valuable insights in these domains.

This report proposes a framework and develops data processing methods to derive statistical indicators from AIS data that enable near real-time analysis of maritime activity for ports and passageways and how they are affected by local and global events or other phenomena. The report first discusses fundamental AIS concepts and then builds on the existing literature on the use of AIS data. Second, it introduces the United Nations Global Platform (UNGP) infrastructure where AIS data can be accessed, processed, and analyzed to produce the indicators used in this report. Third, a framework is proposed to derive indicators from AIS data by identifying Events of Interest (EOIs) and Areas of Interest (AOIs). Lastly, the report shows data processing methods to address common challenges on the use of AIS data such as data quality, big data processing, and identification of geographical boundaries of maritime activity.

These methods are fundamental to the compilation of maritime statistics and can be used to derive statistics beyond those used in this report. Here, indicators are derived for ports and passageways that are important hubs to maritime activity: the Port of Shanghai in the People's Republic of China, Malacca Strait, and Singapore Strait for Asia; the Port of Rotterdam in the Netherlands, Suez Canal, and Strait of Gibraltar for Europe; the Ports of Los Angeles and Long Beach in the United States, and Panama Canal for Americas; and Strait of Hormuz and Bab el-Mandeb Strait for Middle East. Indicators were also derived for areas affected by specific maritime disruptions in recent years: the Port of Nuku'alofa in Tonga where a volcanic eruption occurred in January 2022; the Port of Colombo in Sri Lanka where an economic crisis had been ongoing since 2019; and the Port of Odesa, Dardanelles Strait, and Bosphorus Strait which were affected by the Russian invasion of Ukraine. Such indicators provide valuable insights into the activities of the global shipping industry, enabling governments and policymakers to make more informed decisions. By circumventing delays associated with the release of official statistics, this approach helps promote timely decision-making.

This supplement is the culmination of rigorous study by a range of experts. The special supplement team was led by Mahinthan Joseph Mariasingham under the overall direction of Elaine S. Tan. The core research team included Cherryl Chico, Ed Kieran Reyes, and Amna Gul. Contributing authors of the case studies and the main report include Arpit Kumar and Zhaowen Wang. This report also benefited from the significant contributions of Miro Frances Capili, Kenneth Anthony Luigi S. Reyes, and Eric Suan, who provided both technical and administrative support. Valuable insights and feedback came from Daniel Boller and discussants and participants of two Asian Development Bank events—the 2023 Economists Forum, and the Economic Research and Development Impact Department (ERDI) Seminar on Key Indicators Special Supplement 2023 Workshop: Methodology for Processing Automatic Identification System (Data). This report also received the support of the UN Committee of Experts on Big Data and Data Science for Official Statistics (UN-CEBD) for the UN Global Platform, and feedback from Markie Muryawan and Justin McGurk of the AIS Task Team. The cover of the supplement was designed by Eric Suan. Terry E. Clayton edited the manuscript, while Mark Ganaban led the layout, page design, and typesetting process.

We hope this supplement can help government officials, researchers, and development practitioners in Asia and the Pacific to harness the potential of AIS data as a valuable source of big data. The supplement provides the necessary tools and knowledge to derive insightful information about ongoing events in both local and global maritime shipping, contributing to a more comprehensive understanding of the dynamic nature of global trade.

Albert F. Park
Chief Economist and Director General
Economic Research and Development Impact Department
Asian Development Bank

Abbreviations

AIS	Automatic Identification System
AOI	Area of Interest
DBCV	Density-Based Clustering Validation
DBSCAN	Density-Based Spatial Clustering of Applications with Noise
EOI	Event of Interest
H3	Hexagonal Hierarchical Geospatial Indexing System
IMO	International Maritime Organization
ITU	International Telecommunication Union
LALB	Los Angeles and Long Beach
LSCI	Liner Shipping Connectivity Index
MID	Maritime Identification Digit
MMSI	Maritime Mobile Service Identity
PRC	People's Republic of China
RORO	Roll-on/roll-off
SOG	Speed Over Ground
UNCLOS	United Nations Convention on Laws of the Sea
UNCTAD	United Nations Conference on Trade and Development
UNGP	United Nations Global Platform
UNSD	United Nations Statistics Division
UN-LOCODE	United Nations Code for Trade and Transportation Locations
US	United States
VHF	Very High Frequency
WPI	World Port Index

Highlights

- **The Automatic Identification System (AIS) is an automated tracking system designed to help sea vessels navigate and avoid collisions.** When they are in motion, vessels fitted with AIS equipment send radio messages on their position every 2 to 10 seconds. Other information on the vessel's identification, characteristics, destination, and time of arrival may also be sent.

- **Data from the AIS shows strong potential as an alternative data source for more timely policymaking.** AIS has been used for research on international trade, where it can help determine the most efficient shipping routes and identify supply chain bottlenecks. AIS has also been used in economic analyses to assess port performance, estimate trade flows, monitor fisheries, and estimate maritime carbon dioxide emissions.

- **AIS contains data of high volume, velocity, and variety—attributes that offer several benefits over traditional sources of official statistics.** Since AIS data is available in near real time, it could serve as an alternative source for maritime data until official statistics become available. The statistical offices of the United Kingdom, Ireland, and Denmark have been using AIS data as a supplement until official statistics are published, usually with a lag of 1 to 2 months.

- **Given the promise shown by AIS data, this report aims to develop a framework and methods to derive indicators that leverage its usefulness for unlocking maritime insights.** The framework introduces Events of Interest (EOIs) and Areas of Interest (AOIs) as the fundamental components of these AIS-derived indicators. The methods used address common challenges in using AIS data such as data quality, big data processing, and identification of geographical boundaries.

- **To assess the effectiveness of AIS-derived indicators in capturing changes in port activity, the study uses the Density-Based Spatial Clustering of Applications with Noise (DBSCAN) method to delineate boundaries for key ports.** These ports include the combined ports of Los Angeles and Long Beach (LALB) in the United States, the Port of Rotterdam in the Netherlands, and the Port of Shanghai in the People's Republic of China. The indicators accurately reflected significant events affecting these ports, including port congestion in the ports of LALB throughout 2021, and lockdown measures implemented in Shanghai from March to May 2022.

- **The study finds that AIS-derived indicators closely resemble data from authorities, underscoring the potential of AIS to supplement official maritime statistics.** AIS-derived transit statistics from the Suez Canal and the Panama Canal were nearly identical to figures published by authorities, while AIS-derived statistics for the ports of LALB follow official data trends.

- **AIS-derived indicators for global maritime hubs further reflect the impact of global events on maritime activity.** Extended lockdowns due to coronavirus disease (COVID-19) drove down maritime activity for passenger vessels, while cargo vessels and tankers traffic remained steady. Activities of passenger vessels began to recover toward baseline levels by February 2022, coinciding with the post-pandemic resurgence in economic activity. Regional indicators, meanwhile, suggest the stability of maritime activity amid various economic disruptions, including lockdowns.

- **AIS-derived indicators likewise capture the immediate effects of selected major disruptions on port activities.** For the Port of Nuku'alofa, AIS data accurately reflected a spike in the number of ships from January to February 2022, including naval and rescue ships providing relief following the volcanic eruption of Hunga Tonga–Hunga Ha'apai in Tonga. Likewise, for the Port of Odesa in Ukraine, the substantial decline in ship counts from March 2022 corresponded with the impact of the Russian invasion of Ukraine. Indicators generated for the Bosphorus and Dardanelles Straits—Turkish straits leading to the Black Sea—also exhibited a steep decline in vessel transits in February 2022, signifying the impact of the Russian invasion of Ukraine. For Sri Lanka, though, the Port of Colombo remained resilient despite the ongoing economic crisis.

- **The report's findings make a strong case for the usefulness of AIS data to generate reliable indicators of maritime activity.** While AIS data is not without its quality issues, these are outweighed by the potential benefits for policymaking and research over traditional data sources because of its timeliness and comparability across time and economies. However, users of AIS data should complement it with additional information from trade statistics, economic indicators, and port-specific data to fully contextualize the economic implications of observed trends.

Introduction

It takes months, even years, to compile and publish official statistics due to the time and resources required to collect, process, analyze, and validate relevant data. This lag between data collection and publication can compromise effective economic analysis and policy making which rely on accurate, timely, and reliable information. Recent technological innovations have enabled the exploration of massive datasets known as 'big data' to identify alternative indicators that can illuminate the state and evolution of various economic phenomena, and, therefore, be used to supplement official statistics. Big data is ubiquitous, ranging from more traditional transactional or operational data collected through administrative and commercial sources to non-traditional or innovative data generated or gathered through social networking sites, mobile devices, search engines, and satellite sensors, among others.

One example of big data is the data collected by the Automatic Identification System (AIS), which is a very high frequency radio equipment used by vessels to communicate during navigation. When they are in motion, vessels fitted with AIS equipment send radio messages on their position every 2 to 10 seconds. Other information on the vessel's identification, characteristics, destination, and time of arrival may also be sent. Though originally developed to prevent collisions between vessels, AIS is now gaining popularity for research and analytical applications. The use of AIS data ranges from environmental analysis, where it can provide insights into the movement of vessels and their impact on marine ecosystems, to trade analysis, where it can help determine the most efficient shipping routes and identify supply chain bottlenecks.

AIS data provides certain significant advantages over traditional data sources. First, it offers near real-time updates on vessel positions and movements, thereby providing more timely data for discerning international trade flows. This data innovation based on AIS could help to improve on the current release schedules of official trade statistics, which are usually published with a lag of 1 to 2 months (Asian Development Bank 2022). The availability of more up-to-date data enables better monitoring of economic trends and facilitates timelier responses to market changes. By leveraging the wealth of AIS data, relevant stakeholders can make evidence-based decisions and design effective strategies to optimize trade logistics, monitor supply chains, and enhance overall economic efficiency.

Further, AIS data captures detailed information on individual vessels, including their unique identification, location, speed, heading, and voyage details. This level of granularity allows researchers to examine specific trade routes; track vessel movements between ports; and analyze the activities of different types of vessels, such as cargo vessels, tankers, and passenger vessels. The ability to study trade patterns at such a fine-grained level offers a more comprehensive understanding of the dynamics and complexities of global maritime trade.

AIS data also offers broader coverage over traditional data sources, which often suffer from limited geographical representation and incomplete information. It covers all shipping routes, ports, and maritime zones, providing a comprehensive view of international trade activities. The dataset also provides global coverage of the maritime industry, since AIS equipment is mandatory for all vessels above 300 gross tonnage if engaged in international voyages, cargo vessels with at least 500 gross tonnage if not engaged in international voyages, and all passenger vessels regardless of size. Moreover, AIS data is standardized, making it highly compatible and comparable across different countries and regions. This international comparability allows for cross-country analyses, benchmarking, and identifying best practices in trade facilitation, port efficiency, and logistics management. For example, countries in the Pacific facing data challenges can benefit from AIS data to gain insights into their maritime activities, analyze trade flows, and, eventually, produce economic statistics.

Recent studies have shown the potential of AIS data to provide insights on economic and environmental issues including estimating trade flows, assessing port performance, tracking fisheries, and monitoring maritime carbon dioxide emissions (Arslanalp, Koepke, and Verschuur 2021). AIS-based port call data has also been used to construct trade volume indicators from machine learning algorithms (Cerdeiro, Komaromi, and Liu 2020). Many studies reveal the usefulness of AIS data in identifying disruptions in maritime activities that affect trade (Millefiori, et al. 2021, Verschuur, Koks, and Hall 2021). Similarly, another study examined the use of high-frequency AIS data in developing key indicators for trade monitoring and analysis (Asian Development Bank 2023). Findings suggest that real-time AIS data can help to improve port performance and enhance transparency in supply chains.

This report builds on the existing literature by developing methods for deriving data and producing statistics that can help overcome challenges in big data processing. By leveraging AIS data, the report proposes high-frequency indicators to analyze activities at the port, regional and global levels. **Chapter 1** discusses the literature on the use of AIS data. **Chapter 2** details the fundamental concepts on AIS data related collection, production, and validation processes and frameworks. The chapter also discusses the infrastructure of the United Nations Global Platform (UNGP) where the AIS data required to produce the statistics and indicators in this report were accessed, processed, and analyzed. A customized dataset generated by combining AIS data with Ship Registry data, which contains information about all registered ships in the world, is also introduced. The chapter concludes with a discussion on data quality issues specific to AIS.

Chapter 3 discusses the definitions, concepts and methods related to the preparation and use of AIS data. It defines the concepts of Events of Interest (EOIs) and Areas of Interest (AOIs) and describes how certain key statistics and indicators are derived. Further, it identifies the ports and passageways studied in the report. This chapter also demonstrates a specific method to derive indicators on port activity and maritime highway traffic. Chapter 4 details the procedures for deriving the indicators of interest from AIS data and the sample Python scripts to implement the procedures within the UNGP. It provides a detailed discussion on data preparation, defining areas of interest, the Density Based Spatial Clustering of Applications with Noise (DBSCAN) algorithm, the use of H3 indexing, generation of indicators, and data quality assessment.

Readers interested in the results of the indicators may jump to Chapter 5 which focuses on applications. Using the data generated since 2019, it analyzes global aggregates and explores trends in East Asia, Europe, the Americas, and the Middle East. The implications of the COVID-19 pandemic and the Russian invasion of Ukraine for maritime and port activities are also studied through the lens of AIS data. Chapter 6 presents the indicators produced for three ports affected by disruptions in recent years: Nuku'alofa in Tonga, Colombo in Sri Lanka, and Odesa in Ukraine. The volcanic eruption in Tonga, economic crisis in Sri Lanka, and the Russian invasion of Ukraine precipitated disruptions that invite an AIS based analysis. Chapter 7 concludes by summarizing the report's findings and their relevance, possible use cases for AIS data, and potential improvements to the methods used and indicators presented.

Chapter 1

Literature Review

The extensive digitalization of the global economy over the past two decades, coupled with technological advancements in computing power, has enabled the use of big data. Big data refers to large datasets that cannot be managed and analyzed with standard software, and could be structured, unstructured, or both (Asian Development Bank 2022). A prime example of big data that has gained recent prominence in research applications is the data collected by the Automatic Identification System (AIS). AIS identifies vessels and transmits real-time information on vessel routes via very high frequency radio transponders. AIS transponders send radio messages every few seconds or minutes to other ships and coastal authorities, resulting in a very high volume of data. Aside from the staggering amount of data collected, AIS data has a wealth of information including vessel type, position, destination, size, speed, draught (a possible indication of its load), and navigational status.

Since 2004, the International Maritime Organization (IMO) has required AIS transponders for all ships engaged in international voyages with at least 300 gross tonnage, cargo ships not engaged in international voyages with at least 500 gross tonnage, and all passenger ships irrespective of size. Though initially developed as a navigation safety tool to prevent vessel collisions, the use of AIS data for research and analysis has since gained traction in various fields and is not expected to slow down. AIS data has since been used by institutions in the academe, public sector, and international development, applying the dataset to various use cases and methods.

Several studies underscore the potential of AIS data to generate insights on economic activity, particularly for international trade. Arslanalp, Koepke, and Verschuur (2021) used AIS data to estimate trade flows and assess port performance by constructing daily indicators of port and trade activity. The authors devised an approach to track merchandise trade using vessel data and applied it to Pacific Island countries, which rely heavily on imports and maritime transport for trade. These countries are also highly vulnerable to climate change and disasters, which in turn pose risks to ports and supply chains. The study improves the estimation techniques used in earlier studies by Arslanalp, Marini, and Tumbarello (2019) and Verschuur et al. (2021) by overcoming challenges to estimate cargo payloads, using detailed information on shipping liner schedules to confirm port calls, and applying country-specific information to define port boundaries.

Another study examined the use of high-frequency AIS data in developing key indicators for trade monitoring and analysis (Asian Development Bank 2023). This study presents three applications of AIS data: (i) estimating port calls and waiting time, (ii) suggesting a proxy for trade activities, and (iii) presenting a case study using the data. AIS-based port call data has also been transformed into international trade indicators relevant and meaningful for economic policy. Cerdeiro, Komaromi, and Liu (2020) built indicators of world seaborne trade from AIS radio signals, using different machine-learning techniques to identify port boundaries, construct port-to-port voyages, and estimate trade volumes at the world, bilateral, and economy levels. Findings suggest a good fit with official trade statistics for many economies and for the world in aggregate. The analysis is also extended to sectoral analyses of crude oil trade, and to study events such as Hurricane Maria and the effect of coronavirus disease (COVID-19) lockdowns—measures taken to contain the spread of the novel coronavirus. While the study highlights the potential of AIS data for policymaking, it also emphasizes the importance of economy-specific knowledge to improve model performance for contextualizing economy-specific cases.

Other studies reveal the usefulness of AIS data for identifying disruptions in maritime activities that affect trade. Millefiori et al. (2021) used maritime traffic data from AIS receivers to analyze the effects of the COVID-19 pandemic—and the ensuing lockdowns—on the shipping industry, which accounts for more than 80% of world trade. The authors rely on multiple data-driven maritime mobility indexes to assess ship mobility in each unit of time. The mobility analysis is at the global level and is based on the computation of (i) Cumulative Navigated Miles of all ships reporting their position and navigational status via AIS, (ii) number of active and idle ships, and (iii) fleet average speed. The authors also computed and compared global and local vessel density maps to highlight significant changes in shipping routes and operational patterns and compared mobility levels in 2020 with previous years. In general, the results suggest that trade activity significantly dropped from March to June 2020, when the most severe restrictions were in force. The authors estimate a variation of mobility between –13.77% and –5.62% and for container ships, between –3.32% and 2.28% for dry bulk, between and –9.27% and –0.22% for wet bulk, and between –42.77% and –19.57% for passenger traffic.

Supplement to Official Statistics

Further underscoring its relevance for policymaking, AIS-based trade indicators for measuring trade flows are already being used by governments to supplement traditional data sources. Statistical offices that have used AIS data as an experimental source of port statistics include the United Kingdom Office of National Statistics (UK ONS), Central Statistics Office (CSO) Ireland, and Statistics Denmark. Meanwhile, UK ONS (2019) publishes weekly economic indicators using AIS-derived statistics on port traffic and daily arrivals. Statistics Denmark (n.d.) also publishes a monthly count of port calls based on AIS. CSO Ireland (2022) further showed that AIS-derived port calls accurately capture the trend in official data.

Eurostat, the statistical office of the European Union, established a Working Group on Public Expenditure (WPE). The WPE ESSnet Big Data initiative under the European Statistical System facilitates the use of big data to produce official maritime statistics.

One of the main objectives of the initiative is to improve the quality of current statistics by using AIS data to augment maritime statistics and creating a 'port visits' indicator. Eurostat was specifically only interested in vessels that carried goods. However, since the AIS data do not contain information on what the vessels carry and whether the ship is commercial or not, Eurostat constructed a reference frame that includes three unique identifiers: Maritime Mobile Service Identity (MMSI) number, International Maritime Organization (IMO) number, and a call sign to group vessels. This involved selecting valid MMSI-IMO pairs from static messages of the AIS data and linking MMSIs from the reference frame of vessels to location messages, while selecting specific ports, such as the Winooski port in Poland to Amsterdam in the Netherlands for one day. The results were then compared with official port statistics for validation, revealing a good fit.

UNCTAD: Maritime Indicators

Starting in 2018, UNCTAD publishes an international port calls table every six months. The table features variables such as number of port calls, turnaround times, and the average size and age of vessels across eight ship categories (liquid bulk carriers, LPG carriers, LNG carriers, dry bulk carriers, dry breakbulk carriers, roll-on/roll-off vessels, container vessels, and passenger vessels). As for the number of port calls, only arrivals are defined as port calls, while passenger vessels are excluded. The turnaround time is calculated using the median because of significant outliers due to ship repairs. In the future, it is hoped that AIS data will complement the Liner Shipping Connectivity Index (LSCI) that UNCTAD also maintains, since the index is derived from liner schedules and not actual ship movement.

Global Trade Flows

AIS data becomes more relevant for analysis when combined with Ship Registry data from IHS Markit to obtain positional and temporal information, which can also be disaggregated into ship characteristics. Deriving information on cargo value, which is crucial for estimating trade flows, is less straightforward in AIS due to the absence of cargo-related details such as those found in a ship's bill of lading. This makes it difficult to do a direct analysis on topics such as trade value. However, many studies have devised algorithms that go beyond characterizing ship activity. These open the door to many possibilities such as producing real-time indicators of maritime trade, examining the structure of global maritime trade, and estimating the effect of events on maritime trade volume.

In an International Monetary Fund working paper, Arslanalp, Marini, and Tumbarello (2019) used AIS data port calls for Malta to produce nowcasts on trade activity. The authors identified two indicators using commercial vessels: (i) cargo number, which counts the number of incoming vessels, and (ii) cargo load, which is a derived trade volume index from vessel characteristics and changes in cargo load via changes in the vessel's draught. These two indicators were then validated by benchmarking with high-quality official statistics from the Maltese government, with both indicators providing congruent results though with a few limitations. The study highlights that trade statistics, usually reported with a lag of at least one month by official sources could be estimated in real time using the AIS data. The paper shows that there are many advantages of using AIS data for real-time trade estimates, such as timeliness and granularity.

Using AIS data, Heiland et al. (2019) looked at the 2016 Panama Canal expansion as a natural experiment to derive some insights into global trade patterns using the structure of the shipping network. Knowing that container vessels travel the same routes, the authors developed a method that calculates the fastest routes and characterizes these with descriptive statistics. Using time stamps available in the dataset, direct travel time between two ports can be derived. For all combinations of port pairs, the minimum travel time is determined through Dijkstra's algorithm in a weighted directed network, where edges are direct connections and weights are the direct travel times. To investigate the effect of the Panama Canal expansion, the authors used a difference-in-difference analysis where the dependent variable was quarterly export volume from one economy to another and the explanatory variables were interaction of the time dummy variable and a variable on whether the country-pair is affected by the canal expansion, bilateral controls such as the membership in a free trade agreement, and some other control variables such as geography and language. The authors found there was a 9%–10% increase in trade between country-pairs using the canal after the expansion, and there were welfare gains shared by many economies.

Verschuur, et al. (2021) developed a framework that estimates port-level sector-specific trade flows for many major ports across 180 economies. First, using the April to December 2019 data from the UNGP, the authors manually mapped port areas as polygons. Only port calls related to economic activity were selected, i.e., cargo and tanker vessels and excluding vessels that were likely in port for repairs. Second, two algorithms were constructed to determine the carrying capacity and ship type of observations which had missing information. Third, the authors isolated the effect of domestic trade and transshipment. Domestic trade was removed because it is not part of customs data, while transshipment was accounted for to prevent double-counting and hence the overestimation of trade flows. Fourth, with the adjustments done, the most likely payload was determined using various vessel characteristics and multiple assumptions. Fifth, to disaggregate these results into an economic sector, a conversion table was used that maps a vessel type with an associated economic sector. Finally, in validating the prediction model, it was found that for port-level and sector-level correlation coefficients between monthly trade flows using AIS data and custom data were 0.52–0.96 and 0.79–0.98, respectively, for select large economies. Results were validated against the UN COMTRADE database. COMTRADE contains trade-related information disaggregated by mode of transport, which allowed the authors to consider only maritime trade. Results of the validation showed a good fit with published data, albeit for smaller trade flows. While the study did not create a definitive model to determine trade flows from AIS data, it demonstrated how AIS can be a source of trade flow information for select large economies.

Overall, the extant literature on AIS data underscores its potential as an alternative data source for economic analysis and policymaking, particularly on international trade and climate change. Studies also explore the use of AIS data for other economically meaningful applications. Verschuur, et al. (2021) propose several extensions. First, with a few modifications, AIS data could be used to track tourism through cruise ships as cruise activity resumes post COVID-19 pandemic. It could also be used for regional surveillance and network-level analysis to help forecast trade shocks in a region, given the known transit times between ports, if any of the network components is disrupted. Finally, for economies that rely on maritime trade for imports or exports, AIS data could serve as a supplementary data source for early indicators of economic activity, especially when combined with other satellite data, such as nighttime lights data (Hu and Yao 2019).

Due to the near real-time availability of AIS data, refining methodologies for AIS data processing and interpretation would be particularly useful in times of disasters and other shocks, when there is a high level of uncertainty and traditional indicators become available only after a long delay. The studies cited in this chapter have demonstrated how AIS data—when processed and transformed into economic indicators and interpreted alongside other traditional data sources—can enable policymakers to provide timely responses to economic shocks and monitor the impact of disasters. It could also help regional and international organizations provide timely advice to national authorities impacted by various shocks, and in the longer run, could support regional capacity development efforts to fill data gaps.

Overall, existing studies using AIS data reveal its potential to provide more granular and timely information on maritime statistics. This report develops framework and methods to process and analyze AIS data more efficiently, with a specific focus on deriving maritime indicators potentially relevant for policymaking. In doing so, it aims to extend the body of knowledge on AIS data as an alternative source of official statistics. The study develops methods that address common challenges in the use of AIS data such as data quality, big data processing, and identification of geographical boundaries.

Chapter 2

Automatic Identification System as an Alternative Data Source

This chapter provides a background on important attributes of the Automatic Identification System (AIS) and introduces the UN Global Platform (UNGP), the primary source of AIS data used in this study. These details provide context to the conceptual framework, methodologies, and indicators discussed in the later chapters. Key issues such as data quality and the significance of Ship Registry Data are also discussed to provide context for the methodological framework in the succeeding chapters.

The Automatic Identification System (AIS) is an automated tracking system originally developed to help vessels navigate and avoid collision. The International Maritime Organization (IMO) International Convention for the Safety of Life at Sea (SOLAS) requires vessels of at least 300 gross tonnage on international voyage, cargo vessels of at least 500 gross tonnage not on international voyage, and all passenger vessels to be fitted with AIS equipment. Vessels falling under the IMO requirements use Class A equipment, which has long-range capabilities, a higher frequency of reporting, and specific messaging features. All other vessels not under the IMO regulation may use Class B equipment, which has less stringent operational requirements.

AIS users. AIS equipment users are identified through their unique maritime mobile service identity (MMSI) numbers. The MMSI consists of nine digits, the first three digits of which serve as the maritime identification digit (MID) corresponding to the economy with authority over the vessel's identity. MID values range from 201 to 775. Individual ship stations use the format MIDxxxxxx, where x is a digit from 0 to 9. Group ship station calls, used to identify multiple ships simultaneously, have the format 0MIDxxxxx. Coast stations and other land stations follow the format 00MIDxxxx. Other types are identified by the first digit of the MMSI: 1 for aircraft, 8 for handheld devices, and 9 for aids to navigation, search and rescue, and other free-form identification. According to the International Telecommunication Union (ITU), an MMSI number may be reused if not used for at least two years.

AIS messages. AIS messages sent by vessels are categorized as static, dynamic, voyage-related, or safety-related. Static and voyage-related messages are composed of information on the vessel's identification, characteristics (e.g., type, length, and width), destination, and expected time of arrival. Vessels transmit these messages every six minutes or as requested when there are changes. Dynamic information consists of position reports sent every two to ten seconds when a vessel is in motion, or every three minutes when anchored or moored, depending on the AIS equipment class. Safety-related messages are transmitted as required.

Figure 2.1: Transmission of Automatic Identification System Signal from Vessel to Receiver to User

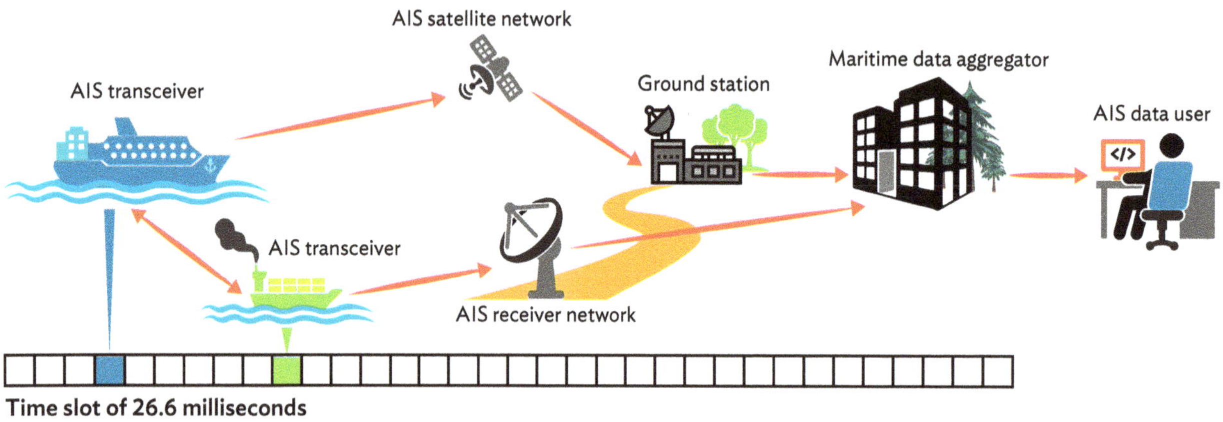

AIS = Automatic Identification System.
Source: United Nations. 2020. AIS Handbook. https://unstats.un.org/wiki/display/AIS/AIS+Handbook (accessed 23 June 2023).

Click here for figure data.

AIS signal transmission. AIS data aggregators receive signals via satellites and AIS-terrestrial receivers. AIS uses time slots of 26.6 milliseconds to simultaneously receive very high frequency signals to avoid interference and loss of communication between vessels. The signals are decoded into messages, which are then processed, cleaned, and transformed for AIS data users (Figure 2.1).

The information contained in AIS meets the criteria of big data posited by Laney (2001) owing to its high volume, velocity, and variety. AIS data provider Spire Global alone produces around 180 million records per day from 68,000 distinct MMSIs. After data processing, about 36 gigabytes of data are generated daily. Traditional data processing tools are thus insufficient to handle its scale and complexity. Big data processing methodologies, which use specialized software and distributed computing systems, are necessary to efficiently manage and extract insights from AIS and similar datasets.

2.1 Big Data Infrastructure in United Nations Global Platform

The United Nations, through the UN Global Platform (UNGP), provides access to AIS data to encourage the use of big data for policy applications with emphasis on measuring progress toward the Sustainable Development Goals. It provides a platform for international organizations, researchers, and statistical offices to collaborate on developing alternative sources of official statistics using big data. UNGP users primarily interacting with AIS data are collectively known as the AIS Task Team.[1]

1 UNGP is available to international development organizations, statistical offices, and researchers interested in studying AIS data and in being part of the AIS Task Team. To get access, an email request should be sent to support@officialstatistics.org.

The AIS data available in UNGP, referred to as UNGP-AIS, is provided by exactEarth, a subsidiary of Spire Global, Inc. The provider collects, cleanses, transforms, and stores live AIS data which can be accessed almost real-time through their application programming interface. UNGP queries and stores live AIS data from position messages every two minutes, and then prepares it for big data processing, incorporating additional features to improve geospatial processes. These features include:

1. ***Parquet storage:*** Parquet is an open-source file format specifically designed for big data processing. Parquet files are columnar, unlike traditional tabular datasets such as comma-separated values, so that only required columns are read and processed. This property makes parquet storage useful for high-frequency data that rapidly increases in size.

2. ***Geospatial indexing:*** Each point of location information, represented by longitude and latitude pairs, has corresponding indices based on H3, a hexagonal hierarchical geospatial indexing system (Uber Technologies 2023). This open-source indexing system facilitates easier data aggregation by converting geospatial processes into one-dimensional functions. H3 divides the Earth's surface into 16 sets of uniquely identified hexagons, with each set representing an H3 resolution. Hexagons from lower resolutions cover a larger area per hexagon, with the lowest resolution averaging around 4 million km^2. Those at higher resolutions cover a smaller area per hexagon, with the highest resolution covering an area of less than 1 m^2.

Historical UNGP-AIS data is available from December 2018 and is updated every four hours. As of May 2023, there were around 4 terabytes of data consisting of 33.5 million records per year on average. Each row corresponds to a position message sent by a single vessel, together with a static message containing details on the vessel's identification, characteristics, and voyage. The UNGP data provider exactEarth decodes fields on vessel type and navigation status to help users interpret values. More information, such as the vessel's flag country, are derived from the raw values. The data includes sixteen H3 indices derived from the latitude and longitude values as additional columns. In total, UNGP-AIS consists of 49 fields. Note that UNGP-AIS is not exhaustive of all types of AIS messages. Messages related to safety are not included.

Table 2.1: United Nations Global Platform-Automatic Identification System Data Dictionary

Field	Sample Value	Description	Message Type
mmsi	258161000	Maritime Mobile Service Identity unique identifier	Position/Static
imo	7712913	International Maritime Organization unique identifier	Static
vessel_name	SEA SALMON	Vessel name	Static
callsign	LHDO	Vessel call sign	Static
vessel_type	Cargo	Vessel type	Derived
vessel_type_code	79	Vessel type code	Static
vessel_type_cargo	No Additional Information	Cargo type	Derived
vessel_class	A	Class A or B	Static
length	56	Vessel length (meters)	Static
width	10	Vessel width (meters)	Static
flag_country	Norway	Flag country derived from MMSI	Derived
flag_code	258	Flag country derived from MMSI	Static
destination	FISHFARMS	Destination	Static
eta	5291800	Estimated time of arrival	Static
draught	7.2	Draught (meters)	Static
longitude	33.37758	Longitude (decimal degrees)	Position
latitude	69.92626667	Latitude (decimal degrees)	Position
sog	10.7	Speed over ground (knots)	Position
cog	316.7	Course over ground (degrees)	Position
rot	0	Rate of turn (degrees per minute)	Position
heading	315	True heading (degrees)	Position
nav_status	Under Way Using Engine	Navigational status	Derived
nav_status_code	0	Navigational status code	Position
source	S-AIS	Satellite or Terrestrial	exactEarth
dt_pos_utc	2023-05-31 05:42:45	Date and time of position message	Position
dt_static_utc	2023-05-31 00:01:11	Date and time of static message	Static
dt_insert_utc	2023-05-31 05:43:51	Date and time of exactEarth data retrieval	exactEarth
vessel_type_main	Fishing Vessel	Vessel type main	Derived
vessel_type_sub	Live Fish Carrier	Vessel type subcategory	Derived
message_type	1	AIS message type	Position/Static
eeid	5019034993509480808	exactEarth ID	exactEarth
source_filename	s3_path/20230531054414.csv.gz	Filename of the source in UNGP's Amazon S3 bucket, where *s3_path* in the prefix of the filename	Derived
H3index_0	8001fffffffffff	H3 index resolution 0 in hexadecimal format	Derived
H3_int_index_0	576495936675512319	H3 index resolution 0	Derived
H3_int_index_1	580986342163349503	H3 index resolution 1	Derived
H3_int_index_2	585489392034906111	H3 index resolution 2	Derived
H3_int_index_3	589992922942799871	H3 index resolution 3	Derived
H3_int_index_4	594496471030562815	H3 index resolution 4	Derived
H3_int_index_5	599000068510449663	H3 index resolution 5	Derived
H3_int_index_6	603503667332513791	H3 index resolution 6	Derived
H3_int_index_7	608007266842443775	H3 index resolution 7	Derived

continued on next page.

Table 2.1 *continued.*

Field	Sample Value	Description	Message Type
H3_int_index_8	612510866461425663	H3 index resolution 8	Derived
H3_int_index_9	617014466088534015	H3 index resolution 9	Derived
H3_int_index_10	621518065715838975	H3 index resolution 10	Derived
H3_int_index_11	626021665343205375	H3 index resolution 11	Derived
H3_int_index_12	630525264970572287	H3 index resolution 12	Derived
H3_int_index_13	635028864597942399	H3 index resolution 13	Derived
H3_int_index_14	639532464225312855	H3 index resolution 14	Derived
H3_int_index_15	644036063852683349	H3 index resolution 15	Derived

Sources: AIS Task Team. 2022. Getting Started Guide wiki. https://code.officialstatistics.org/trade-task-team-phase-1/samplecode/-/wikis/home (accessed 21 June 2023); and United Nations Global Platform for Official Statistics. 2023. AIS Data. https://officialstatistics.org/ (accessed 21 June 2023).

In addition to UNGP-AIS, the UNGP provides various cloud-based developer services to support the AIS Task Team's work.[2] These services include JupyterHub, Gitlab, and Ocean for Apache Spark by Spot. JupyterHub provides an online workspace for data analysis using notebooks. GitLab serves as a platform for project management, version control, data pipelines, and online code collaboration. Particularly for UNGP-AIS, UNGP provides big data technology through third-party service providers AWS Cloud Computing Services and NetApp. Overall, these services lower the barrier to entry to analyzing AIS data.

2.2 Ship Registry Dataset

Combining AIS data with other datasets enhances its value. One useful complement to the AIS is the Ship Registry dataset from S&P Global Market Intelligence, which contains information on a ship's registration, characteristics, ownership, and other details that provide a deeper understanding of specific vessels. Each vessel in the Ship Registry dataset is identified by an IMO number, which is mandatory for all passenger ships of at least 100 gross tonnages, all cargo ships of at least 300 tonnages, and vessels on international voyages regardless of gross tonnage. The IMO number remains consistent over time, making it useful for tracking ships over extended periods. It serves as a more reliable vessel identifier compared to the MMSI, which can change with ownership.

The Ship Registry dataset is available within UNGP starting June 2021. The dataset is updated monthly with details on newly registered ships and ship status changes. As of May 2023, there were at least 250,000 registered ships with 58% or 146,000 in service or commission. The main file of the Ship Registry dataset consists

2 The Statistics and Data Innovation unit (SDI) under the Economic Research and Development Impact Department (ERDI) of the Asian Development Bank (ADB) is an active member of the AIS Task Team. SDI helps maintain the UNGP-AIS, provides technical assistance to other members related to UNGP-AIS data processing, and contributes to the development of notebooks and algorithms to simplify the analysis of AIS data.

of 107 fields, providing comprehensive information on the registered ships. There are 18 supplementary datasets that provide further details on specific fields, such as a detailed vessel classification including the MMSI.[3]

The Ship Registry's vessel type coding system is the most important aspect of the dataset relevant to this report. This coding system classifies ships into 296 vessel types across five levels based on their general category, function, and, in some cases, the nature of cargo carried. At the first level, vessels are categorized into cargo carrying vessels, work vessels, non-seagoing merchant ships, non-merchant, non-propelled vessels, and non-ship structures. The second level further differentiates vessels into cargo vessels, tankers, passenger vessels, fishing vessels, and other types of vessels. These two levels provide a broad classification of ships based on their primary characteristics. The next three levels provide more specific information about cargo carrying vessels, while also offering distinctions for all other types of vessels.

Because of its detailed classification levels, the Ship Registry data can be integrated with UNGP-AIS and used as the main source for identifying the type of vessel. The Ship Registry can supplement AIS data, which follows a different coding system where ship types are only categorized based on the vessel's general classification, and whether it carries dangerous goods, harmful substances, or marine pollutants. AIS vessel classifications associated with trade, which are likely of interest to policymakers and researchers, are limited only to *Cargo* and *Tanker*—the Ship Registry supplements with further classifications such as *Bulk Carrier* and *Container Ship*.

To illustrate the value of integrating these datasets, Table 2.2 lists three sample vessels where details of the vessel vary between AIS and S&P. Vessel *EVER ACE* is categorized by AIS as a cargo vessel. Meanwhile, S&P distinguishes it as a fully cellular container ship—an important distinction as this classification is typically used for reporting trade. Another example is the vessel *OCEANIA*, one of the largest tankers in the world at 234,000 tons. Its specific purpose is fuel storage rather than transporting oil between trading partners. This distinction is not apparent in the AIS data, but the S&P ship type correctly identifies the vessel as Floating, Storage, Offloading (FSO) vessel for oil. While the S&P ship type does not explicitly mention that *OCEANIA* is a tanker, it provides additional information on the vessel's function. Lastly, the vessel *WONDER OF THE SEAS* is categorized in AIS as a passenger vessel, but its S&P ship type classification reveals it is a cruise ship.

3 However, less than half of registered ships have MMSI values. MMSI changes are rare for those ships with MMSIs. Approximately 5% of the ships changed MMSI, with an average of one change every 1.5 years.

Table 2.2: Comparison of Vessel Type Information Between Automatic Identification System Data and S&P Ship Register for Sample Vessels

Item	OCEANIA IMO: 9246633 MMSI: 205753000	EVER ACE IMO: 9893890 MMSI: 352986146	WONDER OF THE SEAS IMO: 9838345 MMSI: 311001033
AIS Vessel Type			
Level 1	Tanker	Cargo	Passenger
Level 2	None	Carrying DG, HS, or MP, IMO hazard or pollutant category	None
S&P Ship Register Vessel Type			
Level 1	Work vessel	Cargo carrying	Cargo carrying
Level 2	Offshore	Dry cargo/passenger	Dry cargo/passenger
Level 3	Other offshore	Container	Container
Level 4	FSO (Floating, Storage, Offloading)	Container ship	Passenger
Level 5	FSO, oil	Container ship (fully cellular)	Passenger/Cruise

AIS = Automatic Identification System; DG = dangerous goods; FSO = floating, storage, offloading; HS = harmful substances; IMO = International Maritime Organization; MP = marine pollutants
Source: United Nations Global Platform for Official Statistics. 2023. AIS Data and Ship Registry Dataset. https://officialstatistics.org/ (accessed 21 June 2023).

BOX 1

Comparison of Vessel Category Information between Automatic Identification System Data and Ship Registry Dataset

Vessel type is one of the static messages contained in AIS. Its accuracy depends on the vessel crew's data entry. For vessels issued an International Maritime Organization (IMO) number, a standardized vessel classification is available in the Ship Registry dataset. To assess the reliability of vessel information in UNGP-AIS, this report compares it with information from the Ship Registry dataset.

First, all vessels in UNGP-AIS from 31 May 2023 and Ship Registry dataset version 26 June 2023 were selected. Since the level of granularity of the categories differs between the two data sources, a main categorization that maps the vessel types for each data source was created. The resulting categories are General Cargo, Tanker, Passenger, Fishing, Work Vessel, Non-Merchant Ships, and Others. Note that cargo vessels are usually broken down into General Cargo, Bulk Carrier, Container Ships, and Other Cargo, such as the one used in the Review of Maritime Transport by the United Nations Conference on Trade and Development (UNCTAD). At this stage, further disaggregation on cargo vessels is not available in the AIS classification.

Vessels from UNGP-AIS are then matched with vessels in the Ship Registry dataset by using a combination of the IMO number, Maritime Mobile Service Identity (MMSI) number, and vessel name. IMO matching assures a correct match, but since this information is not automatically transmitted, some messages do not contain IMO. Because of this, alignment between both MMSI and vessel name are required for a match. From around 219,000 vessels, around 72,000 were matched, of which 87% came from IMO matches and 12% from MMSI matches. Those not matched were largely Fishing, Work Vessels, and Non-Merchant vessels.

Results of the comparison suggest that the vessel classification system in AIS would suffice to yield a generic main categorization of ships, except for Work Vessels. The main categories between AIS and the Ship Registry dataset align for approximately 198,000 or 94% of the vessels. Of the matched entries, majority of those that did not agree on the main categories came from Work Vessels at 66%, followed by Cargo, Fishing, and Passenger at 7–9%. This suggests that the vessel classification in the AIS is sufficient to yield a generic main categorization of ships except for Work Vessels.

Source: Asian Development Bank calculations using United Nations Global Platform for Official Statistics. 2023. AIS Data and Ship Registry Dataset. https://officialstatistics.org/ (accessed 31 August 2023).

2.3 United Nations Global Platform-Automatic Identification System Data Quality

AIS data, like any other data source, is susceptible to data quality issues. These can arise from the raw source and the AIS data provider up to the data processing stage within UNGP. A number of potential data quality issues are described in the succeeding paragraphs. Whenever possible, statistics on the issue are computed using UNGP-AIS, either a random sample or all available data.

1. **Missing AIS signals.**
   - Vessels can turn off their transponders, or vessels can be out-of-range from third-party receivers. For instance, the People's Republic of China (PRC) enforced a new data privacy law in November 2021, reducing the number of signals collected by AIS data aggregators by 45% (Saul and Baptista 2021). For the UNGP-AIS, exactEarth assures that this event had no impact on the data as sources were increased accordingly.

2. **Variations in sampling methods.**
   - In July 2021, exactEarth reduced their sampling frequency for terrestrially-received AIS messages to within a five-minute period according to the type of message due to the large volume of messages received. The UNGP-AIS datasets reduced from 33.5 million rows per day from 2019–2020 to 24.5 million rows per day from 2021 to the present (Figure 2.2).
   - An eight-day back-filling occurred from December 2018 to October 2021 using exactEarth's historical data, which has fewer AIS messages than the live data. The reasons for the back-filling are unknown.

3. **Static messages are prone to error.**
   - Static messages are manually encoded messages which can either be misreported or not reported at all. An example of this is draught, which has been used to estimate cargo volume by computing changes in the measure for a vessel between its arrival at and departure from a port. Arslanalp, Koepke, and Verschuur (2021) note instances when draught had not been updated on leaving port, rendering draught taken during departure from port unreliable. Further, frequency of reporting draught varies across ports (Box 2). Another example is destination, where the recommendation is to report the port of departure and the next port of call using the United Nations Code for Trade and Transport Locations (UN/LOCODE). However, as the field for destination is free text, this formatting is not strictly followed.

Figure 2.2: Count of Daily Automatic Identification System Messages, Unique Maritime Mobile Service Identity, and Unique International Maritime Organization in the United Nations Global Platform

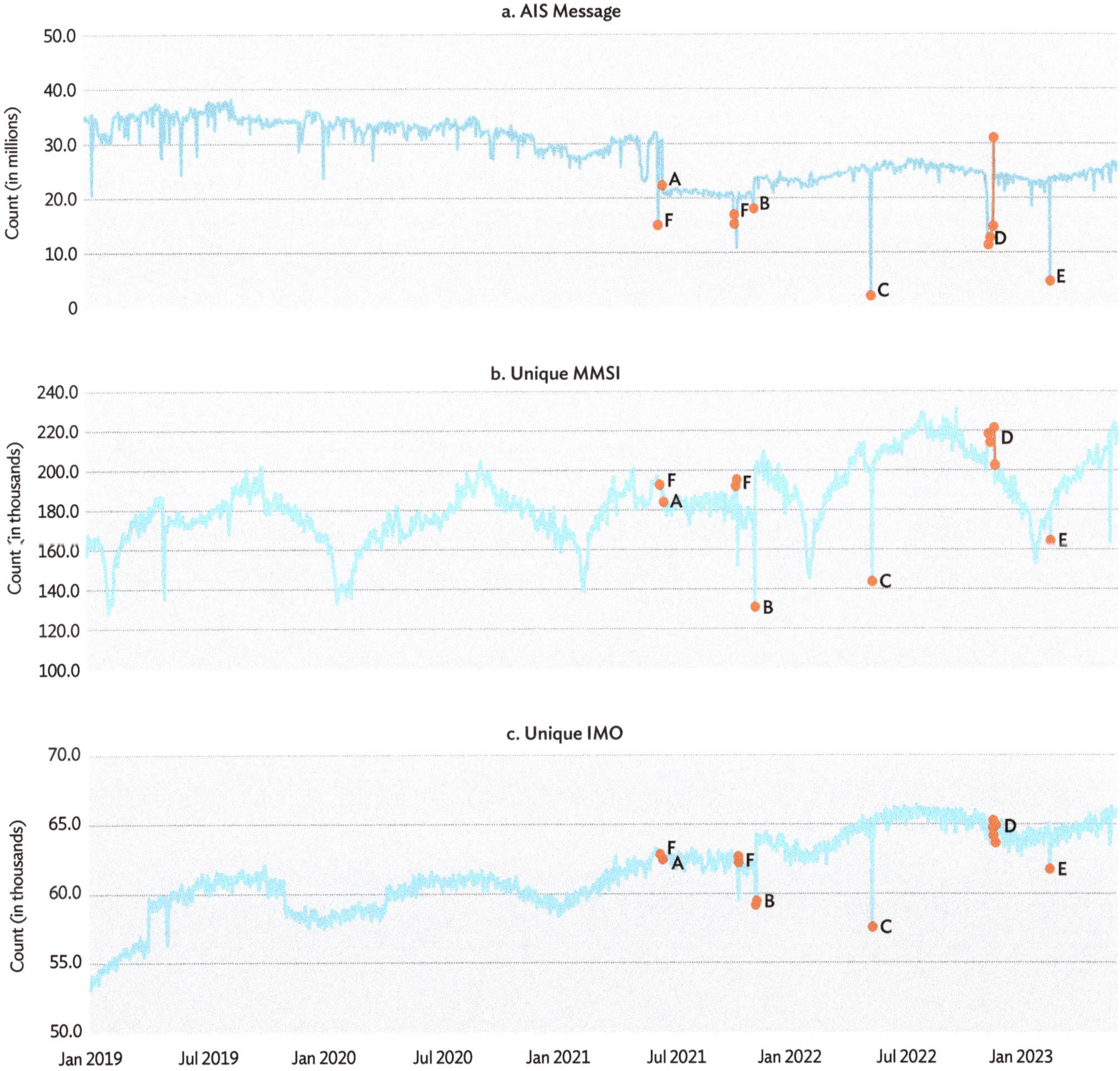

AIS = Automatic Identification System, IMO = International Maritime Organization, MMSI = Maritime Mobile Service Identity.

Notes:

A: 17 June 2021, start of new sampling frequency of exactEarth

B: 7 November 2021, a week after the PRC's new Personal Information Protection Law became effective.

C, E: 12 May 2022, and 14 February 2023, lowest retrieved AIS messages

D: 9–19 November 2022, interruption of UNGP-AIS services due to 2022 AIS Hackathon

F: 10 June 2021, 7–10 October 2021, back-filled data (i.e., not from live data of exactEarth)

Source: Asian Development Bank calculations using United Nations Global Platform for Official Statistics. 2023. AIS Data. https://officialstatistics.org/ (accessed 31 August 2023).

Click here for figure data.

BOX 2

Review of Draught Reporting in Automatic Identification System

A key experimental use case for AIS data is trade estimation, which relies on changes in draught. Defined as the vertical distance between a ship's keel and the waterline, draught has been used to estimate cargo volume by computing changes between arrival at and departure from a port (Arslanalp, Koepke, and Verschuur 2021). Draught is affected by a vessel's cargo load and other factors such as environmental conditions and ballast water tanks. A ship's crew manually enters draught values, which are then transmitted at regular intervals (typically every six minutes or as required by the vessel's AIS equipment class) and stored in AIS as static messages. Port authorities may also ask for draught reporting upon a ship's arrival for operational purposes.

To understand draught in AIS data, reported draught values were compared with yearly vessel arrival counts from 2019 to 2022 for general cargo, tanker, and passenger categories. The analysis was limited to vessels that showed draught changes anytime between arrival and departure in a port. For a proper comparison, the ports of Los Angeles and Long Beach (LALB ports) were selected to represent some of the world's busiest container ports, while the ports of Nuku'alofa, Neiafu and Pangai in Tonga represented small and low traffic ports. Results suggest that most general cargo and tanker vessels arriving at the LALB ports reported draught changes. Meanwhile, fewer than half of vessels at the ports in Tonga reported changes in draught values. Only a few passenger vessels showed changes in draught values across all ports observed.

Count of Arrivals With and Without Change in Draught per Port and Vessel Category

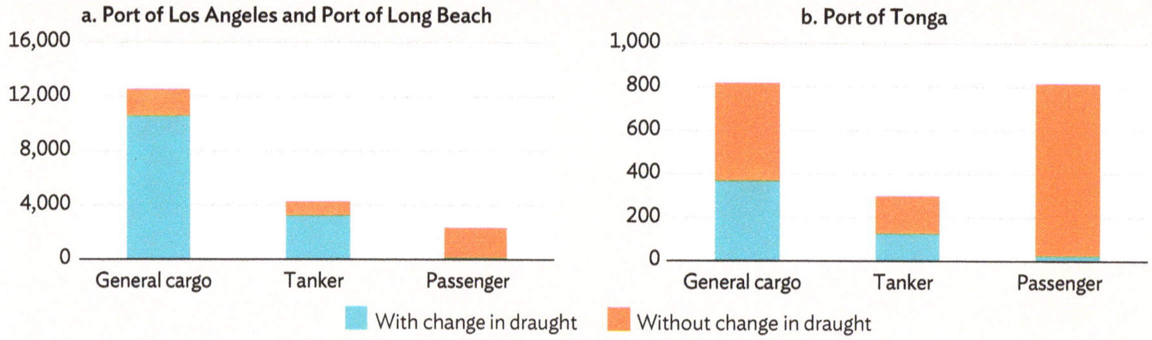

Source: Asian Development Bank calculations using United Nations Global Platform for Official Statistics. 2023. AIS Data and Ship Registry Dataset. https://officialstatistics.org/ (accessed 31 August 2023).

Click here for figure data.

The box plots below depict the distribution of change in vessel draught per vessel category. For the ports of LALB, tankers have the widest interquartile range (IQR), ranging from 0.1 to 3.6 meters with a median value of 1.3 meters. Tankers are followed by general cargo vessels, with IQR ranging from 0.2 to 2.1 meters. For ports in Tonga, the IQR is much narrower for both general cargo vessels and tankers—ranging from 0 to 0.3 meters for general cargo and 0 to 0.2 meters for tankers. For passenger vessels in Tonga, majority did not report changes in draught, explaining the 0 values for all ports in the country.

Distribution of Changes in Draught per Port and Vessel Category

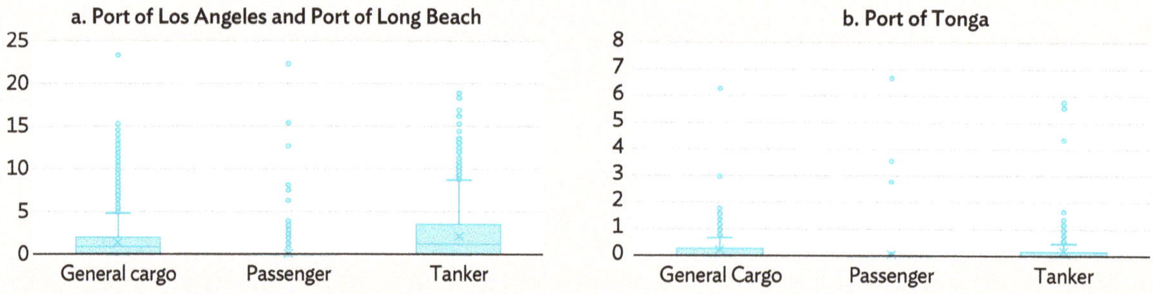

Source: Asian Development Bank calculations using United Nations Global Platform for Official Statistics. 2023. AIS Data and Ship Registry Dataset. https://officialstatistics.org/ (accessed 31 August 2023).

Click here for figure data.

The results shown above indicate that draught reporting tends to vary based on the port and type of vessel. Moreover, manual entry of draught values introduces the possibility of human error. Further research and validation against port authority data is therefore necessary when analyzing AIS-derived draught values.

Reference:

S. Arslanalp, R. Koepke, and J. Verschuur. 2021. Tracking Trade from Space: An Application to Pacific Island Countries. *IMF Working Papers*. 2021 (225). 40. https://doi.org/10.5089/9781513593531.001.

4. **Incorrect MMSI formats.**
    - MMSI is a unique identifier for those operating with maritime mobile service. It is a nine-digit code, including a three-digit maritime identification digit (MID). The first digit of the MID ranges from 201 to 775 and indicates the region of the operator's home economy. However, the position of the first digit in the MID varies from first, second, or third digit. Following the MID rule, approximately 12% of the total unique MMSIs from UNGP-AIS do not follow this format.

5. **Spoofing or anomalies.**
    - There are observed anomalous positions for vessels in the UNGP-AIS. For data from 27 January 2020 to 2 February 2020, MMSIs as high as 200 daily port "visits" (the act of a vessel entering the territorial sea of an economy) were observed—an unlikely occurrence. During the weeks before and after, the number of ports visited by any vessel was 11 per day at most. The reason for this anomaly cannot be easily determined. However, AIS data is known to be susceptible to intentional spoofing (Androjna, et al. 2021) which can also be used to hide maritime activities using fake signals (Triebert, et al. 2023).

Figure 2.2 shows the counts of daily AIS messages, unique vessels according to MMSI, and unique vessels according to IMO from the UNGP-AIS. The graph highlights the drops in AIS data during 2021 to 2023 using markers from points A to F. Point A marks the implementation of the new sampling frequency by exactEarth, resulting in a significant decrease in the number of messages while maintaining the same number of captured vessels. Point B marks a temporary drop in AIS messages influenced by the PRC's new data privacy law (Saul and Baptista 2021). It is worth noting that the number of unique vessels captured has increased from the previous weeks. This may be due to the additional AIS sources used by exactEarth. Points D, and F mark UNGP service interruptions while Points C and E mark days with lowest retrieved messages. Among the observed drops in AIS data, only points B, C, and E had an impact on the derived indicators. Indicators derived for straits of Singapore and Malacca increased after point B. Thus, the periods before and after point B were separated in the analysis. Points C and E caused a sharp decline in the indicators globally. For these dates, the indicators were dropped and treated as missing.

Further, there is a noticeable change in variation in the number of AIS messages from 2022 to 2023 compared to 2019 to 2020. This can be attributed to the improved data processing in UNGP, including an automated data processing pipeline operational since early 2022. As a community-based platform, UNGP does not have established service agreements like the commercial providers of AIS data. However, due to the efforts of the AIS Task Team and United Nations Statistics Division, the services within UNGP are consistently improving, thereby ensuring a reliable and freely accessible platform for studying and analyzing AIS data.

Chapter 3

Framework for Deriving Indicators from Automatic Identification System Data

Making AIS data useful for practical analysis requires translating an extraordinary volume of information into concise indicators. For example, many users would value metrics on maritime highway traffic, port visits, and port congestion. The challenge, however, is that the AIS do not explicitly identify these activities, necessitating a collection of techniques to detect them in the raw data. This chapter describes the conceptual framework that governs these techniques.

The framework proposed in this publication breaks this task into two: detecting *events of interest* (EOIs) and identifying *areas of interest* (AOIs). EOIs are specific maritime incidents or activities that are relevant to a target indicator. AOIs, meanwhile, are the geographic locations where such events occur. These two together help extract the relevant data points from which an indicator may be derived (Figure 3.1). To illustrate, consider an indicator on the volume of traffic in the Port of Shanghai. The EOIs would include all activities that vessels do in ports, such as the loading of cargo, refueling, and anchoring. The AOI, meanwhile, would be the boundaries of the port. The ships that match this EOI–AOI profile comprise the dataset that can then be summarized into an indicator.

Figure 3.1: Components of Automatic Identification System Indicators

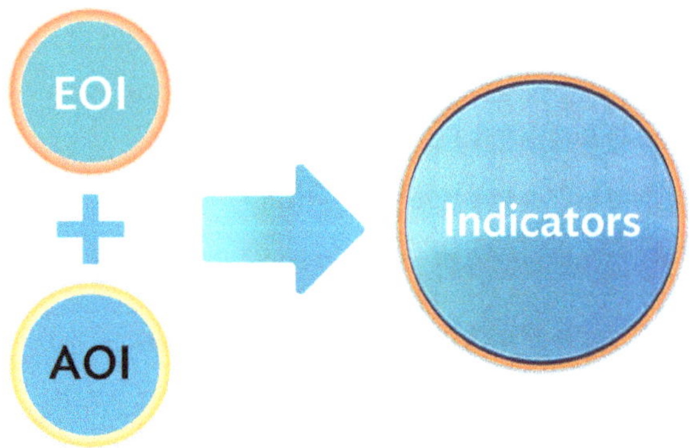

AOI = areas of interest; EOI = events of interest.
Source: Asian Development Bank methodology.

Click here for figure data.

This framework is purposely general to capture a wide variety of phenomena, from trade, to fishing, to tourism. The rest of this report, however, will demonstrate a specific implementation that derives indicators on port activity and maritime highway traffic. Metrics on key ports and passages help paint a picture of maritime activity, particularly in areas where timely data is scarce. This chapter describes how the indicators are defined and which ports and passageways are included in the analysis. The more technical aspects of their implementation are detailed in Chapter 4, while discussions of the calculated indicators are presented in Chapters 5 and 6.

3.1 Port Activity

3.1.1 Identifying Events of Interest and Areas of Interest

The EOIs for port activity indicators are the entry and exit of vessels to and from the port and the assortment of activities that vessels may do in the port. The latter, unfortunately, is not readily available in AIS data, so it is simplified to the act of a vessel being stationary. A high-level categorization of vessel activity may be inferred from its reported type. For example, cargo and tanker vessels are likely to be delivering goods when visiting a port while passenger vessels are likely to be transporting people. However, it is also possible that these types of vessels dock in a port for repair, bunkering, and other activities. Table 3.1 lists the possible categories, including an "Unknown" designation for vessels with missing data.

Table 3.1: Main Category and Subcategory for Vessel Types

Category	Subcategory
tanker	liquefied gas (LPG/LNG) tanker, chemical or products tanker
cargo	bulk carrier, container ship (fully cellular), general cargo, RORO cargo, other
passenger	passenger, cruise ships, RORO cargo
fishing	fishing
work vessel (non-fishing)	towing, pushing, other work vessels
non-merchant ships	non-merchant ships
other	other
unknown	unknown

LNG = liquefied natural gas; LPG = liquefied petroleum gas; RORO = roll on/roll off.
Source: Asian Development Bank.

Defining the AOI for a port is nontrivial. While port infrastructure like docks and wharves are well-defined, anchorage areas off the coastline are less so. These anchorage areas are an intrinsic part of the port since port activities may also be carried out there, as when a larger ship that cannot berth due to draught restrictions transfers its cargo to a smaller ship. Defining the extent of the anchorage area must be done with care as it may change the values of derived indicators.

This report identifies three possible approaches, each with its advantages and disadvantages.

Manual Approach

The most straightforward approach is to manually define the boundaries of the port. If done with expert input or high-quality ground-level data, this could yield the most accurate AOI. However, a significant degree of personal judgment is involved, which can lead to inconsistent decisions when faced with ambiguous cases. This approach also becomes more impractical as the number of ports under consideration rises.

Distance-Based Approach

Adopting a more rules-based approach, the second option sets the boundaries of a port as a pre-defined distance from its center. This has been used both as a means of data reduction (Central Statistics Office 2022) and as port boundaries (Noyvirt, et al. 2019, Arslanap, Marini and Tumbarello 2019). The United Nations Convention on Laws of the Sea (UNCLOS) sets a country's territorial zone as 12 nautical miles (22 km) from its low-water coastline, so 22 km is a good candidate for setting the boundary distance. The implementation in this report draws a square centered at the port's coordinates, with the shortest distance of the center point from the square's side being 22 km. This approach removes personal judgment and can be scaled up easily. However, no guarantee can be made over how accurate the resulting boundary will be. The 22 km limit may be large enough to capture adjacent ports. Moreover, the boundaries of ports may change over time due to expansions and closures.

Figure 3.2 demonstrates how a 22 km bounding box around the Port of Colombo, Sri Lanka would look like. Overlaid is a heatmap of points depicting stationary vessels as collected from AIS messages in 2019. While the box adequately captures the entirety of the port's berthing areas (3.5 km bounding box) and anchorage areas, a case can be made that it includes large areas that should not be part of the port, such as nearby terminals, and vessels transiting. It is also clear that setting a boundary manually would be fraught as the extent of the anchorage area is ambiguous.

Cluster-Based Approach

Combining the benefits of the case-by-case consideration of the manual approach and the procedural method of the distance-based approach is one that employs algorithmic techniques to set port AOIs. Specifically, boundaries are inferred based on the identification of clusters in AIS messages, around which a convex polygon is drawn to demarcate the AOI. This approach has been used to detect anchorages (Fuentes and Adland 2020) and capture potential changes in port boundaries (Arslanap, Marini, and Tumbarello 2019). It has been of particular use for Pacific Island countries due to their small size (Arslanalp, Koepke, and Verschuur 2021). The advantage of a cluster-based approach is that it sets port boundaries according to actual ship behavior, which is not only potentially more accurate but also more responsive to port expansions and closures. It is easier to scale up than the manual approach, though since machine learning is involved, computational resources can be a limiting factor. An element of judgment also cannot be avoided due to the selection of hyperparameters. See section 4.2.3 for more details on implementation.

Ultimately, none of the three approaches are perfect. The best practice is to use the approach that suits the research question, data availability, and resources at hand. This report generally employs variations of the cluster-based approach, with a shift to the distance-based approach to derive global aggregates.

Figure 3.2: Heatmap of Automatic Identification System Locations Within 22 km Square Boundary from the Port of Colombo

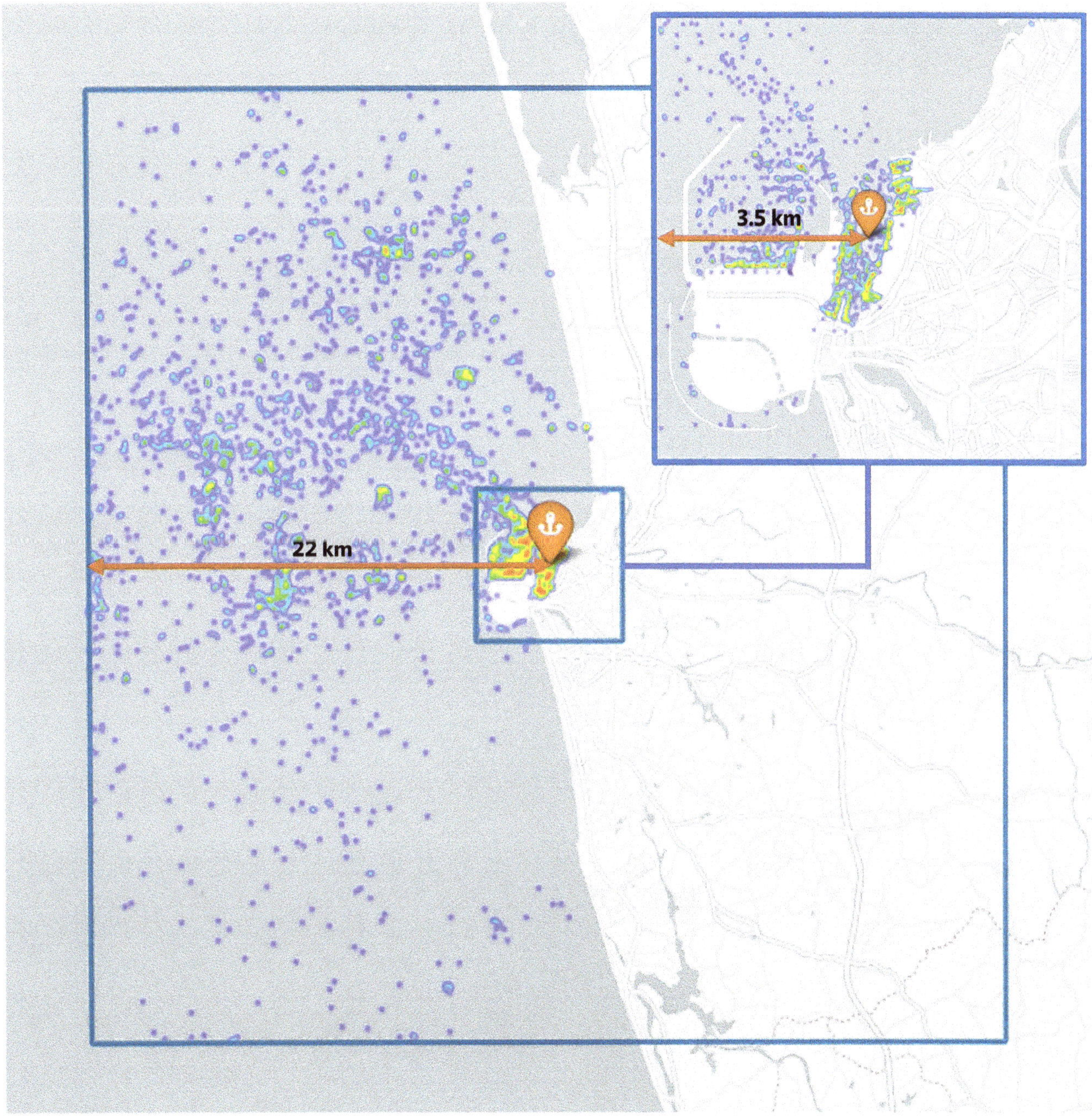

km = kilometer.
Notes: The heatmap is generated from AIS messages sent by all vessels with SOG < 1 knot for 2019 within 22 km distance from a location within the port represented by the orange marker. The color gradient from blue to red represents levels of intensity of the number of AIS messages. Blue indicates areas with a low number of messages and red are areas with a high number of messages.
Sources: Asian Development Bank calculations using United Nations Global Platform for Official Statistics. 2023. AIS Data. https://officialstatistics.org/ (accessed 31 August 2023); Maps are generated using V. Agafonkin, et al. 2023. Leaflet / Leaflet v.1.9.4. https://leafletjs.com/; OpenStreetMap. https://www.openstreetmap.org/copyright.; and Carto. https://carto.com/attribution/.

Click here for figure data.

3.1.2 Indicators

Operationalizing this report's measure of port activity are three indicators: (i) the count of unique vessels in a port, (ii) the number of arrivals in a port, and (iii) the median time spent by vessels in a port.

Count of Unique Vessels

A straightforward measure of port activity is to simply count the number of unique vessels that dock in a port over a given period. The higher this number, the busier the port. Since this measure does not consider the rate or timing of arrivals and exits, the only EOI to take note of is the act of a vessel being stationary. Consequently, vessels that enter the AOI but do not stop are not counted; these may merely be passing through.

Identification of unique vessels is done through their MMSI number. Each vessel found stationary in the AOI is counted once and only once for the chosen time period, even if it moves within the AOI or if it exits and reenters the AOI. This indicator is a stock rather than a flow, so vessels exiting the AOI do not reduce the count. Figure 3.3 visualizes various scenarios that show how the indicator works. Suppose the time period is one day. On day 1, two vessels—ship 1 and ship 2—enter the port boundary, hence the indicator value is 2. On the second day, ship 1 stays, ship 2 leaves, and ship 3 enters and leaves. The indicator for the day is 3. On the third day, ship 1 leaves and no new ship enters. The indicator for the day is 1.

Figure 3.3: Method for Counting Port Indicators

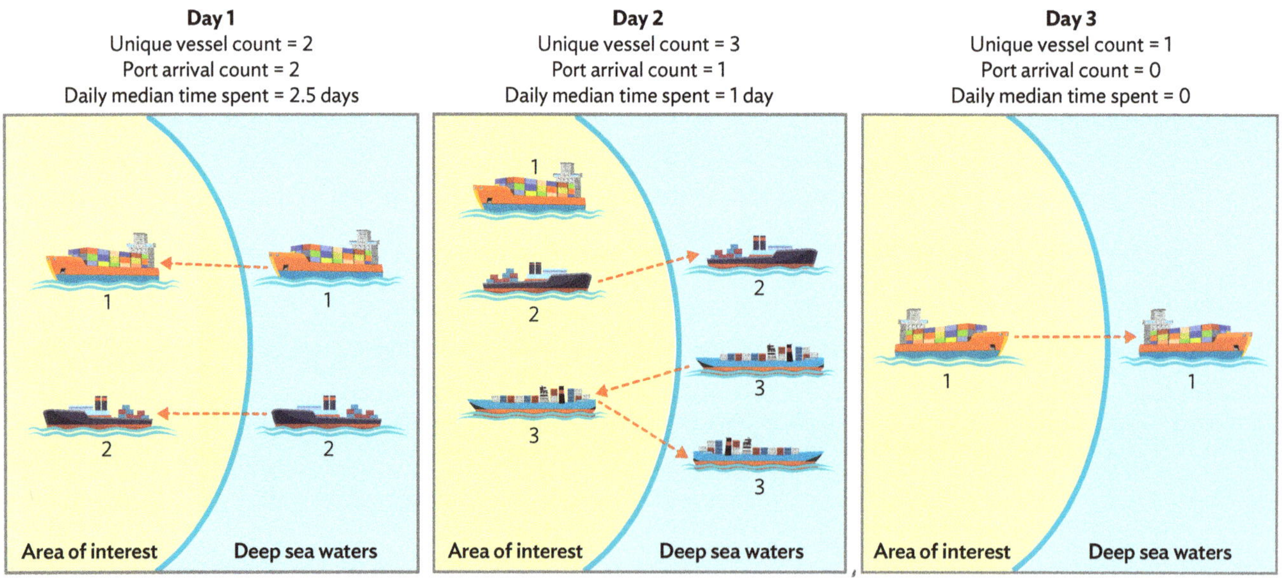

Notes: The areas of interest (AOIs) are represented by the blue line, where the area on the left is within the AOI and area on the right is outside the AOI. All vessels are stationary.
Source: Asian Development Bank methodology.

Click here for figure data.

Count of Arrivals

Complementing the stock count of docked vessels is the flow count of vessel arrivals. There are now two EOIs: vessels entering the port boundary and vessels becoming stationary within the port boundary. Using the same scenarios illustrated in Figure 3.3, on day 1, ships 1 and 2 enter the port boundary, putting the count of arrivals at 2. On the second day, ship 1 stays, ship 2 leaves, and ship 3 enters. The count of arrivals is 1. On the third day, ship 1 leaves and no new ship arrives. The count of arrivals is 0.

Because it is now important to know the precise moment a vessel enters the AOI, it is necessary to track vessel movements not only in the AOI but also in some buffer region right outside the AOI. The details of this movement aggregation method are given in the Appendix.

Median Time Spent in Port

Vessel turnaround time is the most influential factor in port efficiency and performance (Karnoji, Gurudev, and Siddaramaiah 2021). From the perspective of supply chain managers, port authorities, policymakers, and other stakeholders, information on turnaround time is useful for planning infrastructure and improving port operations. For this indicator, the EOIs are the vessel's entry to, halt in, and exit from the AOI. Its entry and exit bookend the total time it spent in the port, while the requirement that it stops ensures that it was not simply passing through. To aggregate durations, the median time spent of all vessels that entered on the reference date is taken. By construction, this indicator would change as these vessels make their exit.

To illustrate, consider again the scenario in Figure 3.3. Ship 1 arrives on day 1 and spends 3 days in port. Ship 2 also arrives on day 1 and spends 2 days in port. Ship 3 arrives on day 2 and spends 1 day in port. The median time spent is aggregated per day of arrival. Thus, the median time spent in port for day 1 is 2.5 days, and 1 day for day 2. The time spent in port for each ship needs to be observed until the departure day. However, a partial indicator can be computed based on the time spent by the ship up to that point. The indicator is then updated in the succeeding days.

3.2 Traffic Along Maritime Highways

3.2.1 Identifying Events of Interest and Areas of Interest

Notteboom, Pallis, and Rodrigue (2022) define maritime chokepoints as strategically important maritime passageways that may have limitations in terms of capacity due to their narrowness or shallow depths, and where disruptions can have a significant impact on the global economy. Naturally occurring passageways are usually called straits (e.g., the Strait of Malacca) while artificial passageways are usually called canals (e.g., the Suez Canal). Vessels cross passageways to get from port to port; measuring their traffic can therefore supplement port-level indicators to provide a fuller picture of global maritime activity.

The EOIs for passageways are a vessel's entry at one end and its exit at the other. No distinction is made whether they stop along the way or not. Vessels that enter at one end but then turn around and exit at the same end are *not* considered to have crossed that passageway.

The AOI for passageways needs to be able to capture the transit of vessels. A maximalist approach would set the AOI across the whole of the passageway to be able to track the complete movement of all entering vessels. This, however, is computationally intensive and difficult to scale. A more strategic approach would set AOIs at key sections of the passageway. Two approaches are employed in this report. The first sets an AOI at each mouth of the passageway, with the actual boundaries determined by a cluster-based approach to include anchorage areas (see section 3.1.1). AOIs at the mouths tend to be more accurate since they verify that a vessel has both entered and exited the passageway. However, they become less feasible if the passageway has very wide or even undefined mouths.

The second approach sets just one AOI at the narrowest point near the middle of the passageway. The reasoning is that any vessel detected here can be assumed to be in transit through the passageway. Having to monitor just one AOI is computationally more efficient. A disadvantage of this approach, however, is that the AOI may miss the AIS messages sent by passing vessels, as depicted in the scenario in Figure 3.4.

This report favors setting AOIs at the mouths for passageways, only turning to setting AOIs at the midpoint whenever the former is not feasible.

Figure 3.4: Sample Area of Interest and Vessel Travel Path for a Passageway

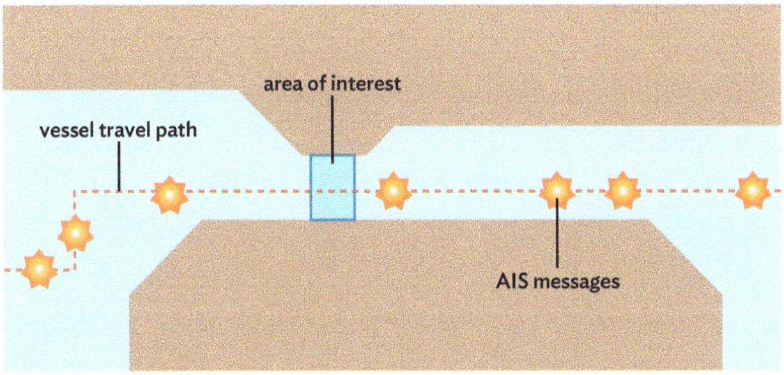

AIS = Automatic Identification System.
Source: Asian Development Bank visualization.

Click here for figure data.

3.2.2 Indicators

Three indicators for passageways are computed: (i) the count of unique vessels (for all passageways), (ii) count of transits (for the Suez Canal and the Panama Canal only), and (iii) median time spent by vessels (for the Suez Canal and the Panama Canal only). The associated measurement principles mirror those related to port activity indicators (see section 3.1.2).

3.3 Ports and Passageways Selected for Analysis

Two considerations determined the selection of ports and passageways for which indicators are computed in this report. First, given the objective of providing proof-of-concept for utilizing AIS data, it is useful to present indicators on the world's major ports and maritime highways to allow for validation with plenty of established datasets. To this end, the largest ports based on the World Shipping Council (2019) and ports with the highest connectivity to different regions of the world (Hoffman and Hoffman 2020) were chosen. The top three that emerged were the ports of Shanghai, Rotterdam, and Los Angeles.[4] Fortuitously, they also have a good geographic spread, representing Asia, Europe, and the Americas, respectively. To complement these, indicators on major passageways in each region were also computed, namely: the Malacca and Singapore straits for Asia, the Suez Canal and the Strait of Gibraltar for Europe, and the Panama Canal for the Americas. In addition, the straits of Hormuz and Bab el-Mandeb were also included due to their centrality in the global trade of oil. These passageways are similar to the chokepoints identified by Notteboom, Pallis, and Rodrigue (2022) and Komiss and Hunzinger (2011).

4 Due to their proximity, the ports of Los Angeles and Long Beach are treated in this report as one port.

The second consideration was to find examples where the granular and real-time features of AIS data can be showcased. These would involve dramatic and unexpected disruptions to maritime traffic for which official data often appear with a substantial lag. Three such cases were considered, all of which occurred or intensified in 2022: the Russian invasion of Ukraine, the Sri Lankan economic crisis, and the Tonga volcanic eruption, respectively representing disruptions arising from military conflict, economic turbulence, and disasters. Their corresponding ports and passageways are the Port of Odesa, the Dardanelles Strait, and the Bosphorus Strait; the Port of Colombo; and the Port of Nuku'alofa.

The selected ports and passageways and the motivation behind choosing them are summarized in Table 3.2. They are also shown on a map in Figure 3.7.

Table 3.2: List of Selected Ports and Passageways

Motivation		Ports	Passageways
Major hubs of maritime activity	Asia	Shanghai	Malacca, Singapore
	Europe	Rotterdam	Suez Canal, Gibraltar
	Americas	Los Angeles and Long Beach	Panama Canal
	Middle East (oil)		Hormuz, Bab el-Mandeb
Cases of maritime disruptions	Military conflict	Odesa	Dardanelles, Bosphorus
	Economic turbulence	Colombo	
	Disaster	Nuku'alofa	

Source: Asian Development Bank.

Figure 3.5: Location of Selected Ports and Passageways

Sources: Google Maps. Passageways Locations. https://www.google.com/maps (accessed 21 June 2023); K. Jordahl et al. 2020. Geopandas/geopandas: v0.12.1 (Version v0.12.1). Zenodo. http://doi.org/10.5281/zenodo.3946761.; and National Geospatial-Intelligence Agency. 2020. World Port Index (Pub 150) Database. https://msi.nga.mil/Publications/WPI (accessed 21 June 2023).

Click here for figure data.

Chapter 4

Data Processing

This chapter describes the process behind deriving the indicators discussed in Chapter 3 and provides sample Python scripts to help readers implement the procedures within the UN Global Platform (UNGP). The scripts use two libraries tailored for AIS data within the UNGP: the ais library built by the AIS Task Team, and the aiski library developed for this publication. The sample scripts, reference files and derived indicators are accessible through the aiski repository in the UNGP Gitlab.[5] Intermediate data outputs are stored in the UNGP's cloud storage for AIS users. Instructions for using these are included in the aiski repository.

4.1 Data Preparation

In AIS data, the events of interest (EOIs) for ports and passageways are inferred by combining information on the MMSI, speed, location, and movement. Specifically, the MMSI number is used to identify signals coming from individual vessels, the speed and location as an indicator of existence of activity, and movement to capture the entirety of the activity. The steps used to identify the EOIs are described in the succeeding paragraphs.

First, messages coming from individual vessels are gathered. UNGP keeps records from all types of AIS including messages from coast stations, aids to navigation, aircraft, mobile radios, and search and rescue. To get messages coming from individual vessels, the MMSI should be 9 digits, with the first three digits between 201 and 799.

The second step is to determine if the messages occurred within an area of interest (AOI). The location of the message should exist within the geographic boundary of the AOI. In UNGP-AIS, geospatial processes are implemented through H3 indices. The H3 geospatial indexing system maps the surface of the Earth to hexagons with varying resolutions (see section 2.1). Thus, all messages have a location data and a set of H3 indices. To check if the message occurred inside the AOI, the H3 index of the message should be included in the H3 indices that cover the AOI. Otherwise, the message occurred outside of the AOI.

The resolution of the H3 index should be carefully chosen such that the desired accuracy of the location is retained. To illustrate, consider a square AOI and two messages A and B (Figure 4.1). The hexagons serve as the H3 indices covering the AOI and messages. The small hexagons are H3 indices with high resolution, while the large hexagons have low resolution. Figure 4.1 makes clear that A is inside the AOI while

5 https://code.officialstatistics.org/adb-data-team/aiski.git.

Figure 4.1: Illustration of High and Low H3 Index Resolution

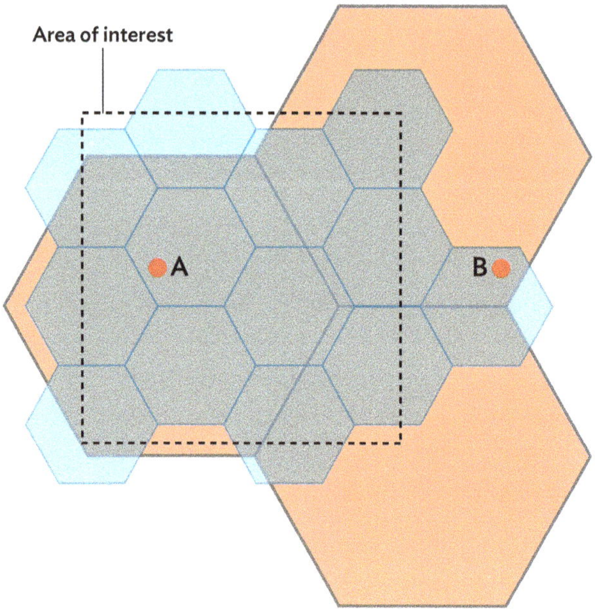

Source: Asian Development Bank visualization.

Click here for figure data.

B is not. Using the high-resolution indices, the hexagons covering the AOI also cover A and exclude B, which is the desired outcome. However, when the low-resolution indices are used, the hexagons that cover the AOI cover both A and B. Thus, the high resolution H3 indices should be used. This publication uses either resolution 8 or 9, where each hexagon has an average side length of approximately 531 m and 201 m respectively.

The third step is to determine if the message within the AOI occurred during an activity. For ports, the activities generally happen when a vessel reports a navigational status of 'At Anchor' or 'Moored'. For passageways, the vessel should be in transit or 'Underway'. However, this information is manually updated, introducing the possibility of human error. An alternative is to look at the vessel's speed over ground (SOG) as vessels that are 'At Anchor' or 'Moored' will generally be stationary, and those that are 'Underway' will generally be moving.

Table 4.1 shows the distribution of SOG per navigational status from 50 randomly sampled dates between 1 December 2018 and 30 April 2023 using data from UNGP-AIS. At the 95th percentile, the SOG values for 'At Anchor' and 'Moored' are at least one knot, and at the 99th percentile the values increase to at least nine knots. Based on this, a cutoff of one knot is chosen for this publication—any vessel with SOG of less than one knot is considered stationary and moving otherwise.

Table 4.1: Distribution of Speed Over Ground of Vessels per Navigational Status

	Speed Over Ground (knot) Quantile					
Navigational Status	50%	75%	90%	95%	99%	99.9%
Moored	0.0	0.0	0.1	3.0	10.6	19.5
At anchor	0.0	0.1	0.3	1.0	9.1	14.2
Aground	0.0	0.1	6.4	9.0	13.3	21.9
Restricted maneuverability	0.1	1.2	5.0	7.6	11.8	18.6
Not under command	0.8	2.0	7.7	11.0	15.1	25.1
Underway sailing	0.1	5.6	10.4	12.3	16.2	26.2
Underway using engine	9.0	12.3	15.0	17.0	20.3	28.6
Engaged in fishing	2.3	5.3	9.0	10.4	12.5	25.0

Source: Asian Development Bank calculations using United Nations Global Platform for Official Statistics. 2023. AIS Data. https://officialstatistics.org/ (accessed 31 August 2023).

The steps shown are sufficient to create the count of unique vessels indicator. For the indicator that relies on movement, i.e., port arrivals and passageway transits, the final step involves grouping the messages according to the occurrence of the EOI. A single event starts when the vessel enters the AOI and ends when it leaves. The next time a vessel enters the AOI, it is considered another event. Thus, it is necessary to track the movement of the vessel overtime in two locations, the AOI and the surrounding area outside of the AOI, referred to here as non-AOI.

The non-AOI is necessary to observe the entry and exit of the vessel to the AOI. Tracking the movement for ports is straightforward, a movement from a non-AOI to an AOI means an entry, and the movement from an AOI to a non-AOI means an exit. For passageways, each opening must have an AOI and a non-AOI. To track the movement for passageways, the vessel must move from a non-AOI to an AOI of opening 1 for entry, then move from an AOI of opening 1 to an AOI of opening 2 to establish a transit, and then move from an AOI to a non-AOI of opening 2 for exit. Consecutive AIS messages from a single vessel occurring within an AOI will be treated as a single event. For this publication, the MMSI is used as the unique identifier of the vessel since not all vessels have IMO and the possibility that the MMSI changes during an event is assumed to be small.

Python Script 4.1 shows a sample implementation in Python of the data preparation steps for a given port using UNGP-AIS from 1–31 January 2023. The pre-requisites are the port.json and buffer.json which refers to the port AOI and non-AOI respectively. The resulting data consists of AIS messages from individual vessels that are within the AOI and non-AOI boundaries, with additional fields to indicate which boundary the message is contained, if the vessel is stationary, and the group number for the event.

Python Script 4.1: Data Preparation for Ports

Script

```
1   import json
2   from pyspark.sql import functions as F
3   from ais import functions as af
4   from aiski import functions as afki
5
6   aoi_json = json.load(open(‘port.json’))
7   naoi_json = json.load(open(‘buffer.json’))
8
9   hex_df = af.polygon_to_hex_df([(‘aoi’, aoi_json),
10                      (‘nonaoi’, naoi_json) ], 8) \
11          .drop_duplicates(subset=[‘hex_ids’]) \
12          .rename(columns={‘hex_ids’: ‘H3_int_index_8’,
13                      ‘polygon_name’: ‘area’})
14  hex_sdf = spark.createDataFrame(hex_df)
15
16  sdf = af.get_ais(spark, start_date=’2023-01-01’, end_date=’2023-01-31’) \
17          .filter(F.col(‘mmsi’).between(201000000,799000000))
18
19  aoi_naoi_sdf = sdf.join(hex_sdf, how=’inner’, on = ‘H3_int_index_8’) \
20    .withColumn(‘stationary’, F.when(F.col(‘sog’)<1, F.lit(‘Y’)) \
21                .otherwise(F.lit(‘N’)))
22
23  movement_flag_sdf = afki.assign_movement(
24    sdf=aoi_naoi_sdf,
25    ship_identifier_cols=[‘mmsi’],
26    movement_orderby_cols=[‘dt_pos_utc’],
27    movement_groupby_cols=[‘area’])
```

Description

1–4	Import the necessary libraries.
6–7	Read the AOI and non-AOI into json objects. Note that for ports, there is only 1 AOI and non-AOI.
9–13	Using the polygon_to_hex_df function of ais library, get the H3 resolution 8 indices that cover the AOI and non-AOI. Each H3 index should belong to either AOI or non-AOI. The function returns a pandas dataframe contains columns H3_int_index_8 and area.
14	Convert the pandas dataframe into a spark dataframe.
16–17	Using the get_ais function of ais library, get the AIS messages from 1–31 January 2023 from individual vessels.
19–21	Get only AIS messages with the same H3 index as the AOI and non-AOI and create a new column stationary to mark if the message is from a stationary vessel.
23–27	Using the assign_movement function of aiski library, assign each message to an event, where an event consists of consecutive AIS messages of a single MMSI in the same area (AOI or non-AOI).

Source: Asian Development Bank.

For passageways, depending on the indicator, additional AOIs may be needed. For count of unique vessel indicator, the above script works. However, for passageway transit, an AOI and a non-AOI are needed for each opening of the vessel. The corresponding changes in the script are in Python Script 4.2.

Python Script 4.2: Data Preparation for Passageways, Changes from Ports

Script

```
1  aoi1_json = json.load(open(‘north_aoi.json’))
2  naoi1_json = json.load(open(‘north_naoi.json’))
3  aoi2_json = json.load(open(‘south_aoi.json’))
4  naoi2_json = json.load(open(‘south_naoi.json’))
5
6  hex_df = af.polygon_to_hex_df([(‘aoi_1’, aoi1_json),
7                      (‘nonaoi_1’, naoi1_json),
8                      (‘aoi_2’, aoi2_json),
9                      (‘nonaoi_2’, naoi2_json),
10                    ], 8) \
11         .drop_duplicates(subset=[‘hex_ids’]) \
12         .rename(columns={‘hex_ids’: ‘H3_int_index_8’})
13 hex_df[[‘area’,’sub_area’]] = hex_df[‘polygon_name’].str.split(‘_’,expand=True)
```

Description	
1–4	Read the AOI and non-AOI into json objects. Each opening has a set of AOI and non-AOI.
6–12	Using the polygon_to_hex_df function of ais library, get the H3 resolution 8 indices that cover the AOI and non-AOI. Each H3 index should belong to either AOI or non-AOI. The function returns a pandas dataframe contains columns H3_int_index_8 and area.
13	Create columns ‘area’ and ‘sub_area’ . The first refers to whether the area is an AOI or a non-AOI, and the latter whether the area is in a specific opening.

Source: Asian Development Bank.

Integration with Ship Registry Data

The Ship Registry data is used as the main source for identifying the type of vessel. To match the vessels in AIS data with Ship Registry data, at least two out of the three unique identifiers for the vessels should match. These identifiers are MMSI, IMO, and vessel name. For vessels without a match in Ship Registry, the vessel type in AIS data is used.

4.2 Areas of Interest

Three approaches are applied to identify the AOI: manual, distance-based, and cluster-based. The choice of approach varies according to the indicator and level of aggregation. For indicators of specific ports, the cluster-based approach is chosen as it produces the most precise boundary among the approaches that are reflective of the activity happening within the port and its surrounding nearby waters. For global aggregate of port indicators, the distance-based approach is used to generate AOI for all ports (> 3,700). This approach is chosen for its simplicity and efficiency in generating large volumes of AOIs. While the boundaries are not as accurate as cluster-based AOIs, the impact of the inaccuracy at the port level is reduced when aggregated to the global level.

For passageways, the narrowest areas are determined manually. This AOI is used for the count of unique vessel indicator. In addition, for canals, because it has narrow openings and because disruptions on its activity can cause buildup of vessels in the surrounding waters of the opening, such as what happened in the Suez Canal blockage, the AOIs for the openings are also generated using the cluster-based approach.

4.2.1 Manual Area of Interest

In choosing the narrowest area of the passageways, the following are taken for consideration: (i) the width should be one of the narrowest widths of the entire passageway, (ii) the area should not cover any nearby ports, and (iii) the length should be sufficient to capture the signal sent while moving. Figure 4.2 illustrates the manual AOIs for all passageways used in this publication. Note that for the Suez Canal and the Panama Canal, the AOIs cover majority of the passageways because their widths are quite narrow (< 1 km).

Figure 4.2: Narrowest Areas of Interest for Passageways

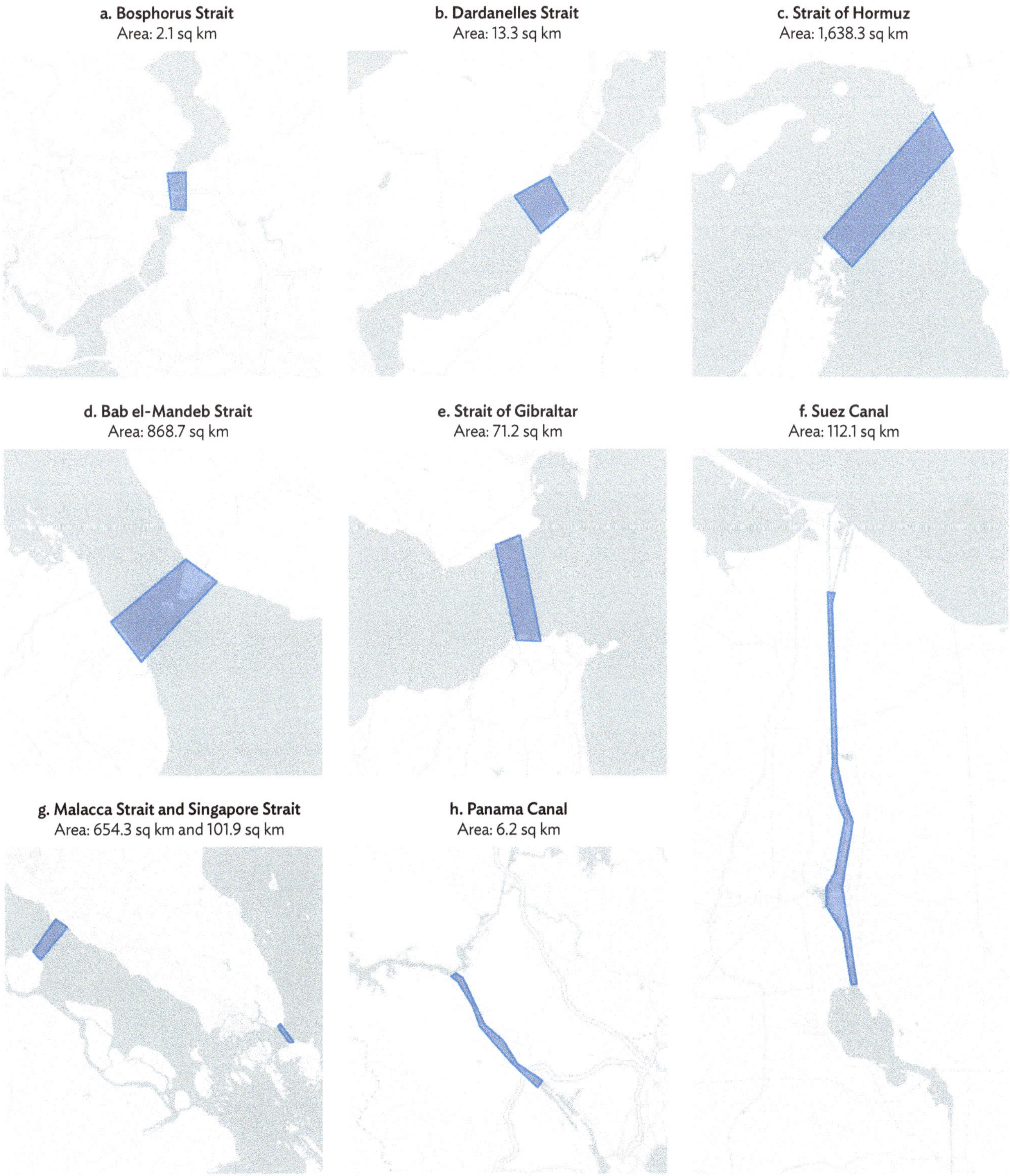

sq km= square kilometer.
Notes: Images are not proportional across maps. The areas are computed automatically from geojson.io.
Sources: Asian Development Bank geographic boundaries using geojson.io; Maps generated using T. Macwright, et al. 2023. Mapbox/geojson.io. https://geojson.io/ (accessed 31 August 2023); MapBox https://www.mapbox.com/about/maps/; and OpenStreetMap. https://www.openstreetmap.org/copyright.

Click here for figure data.

4.2.2 Distance-based Area of Interest

The list of ports and their geographical coordinates are taken from the World Port Index database. A square is drawn centered on the port location. The shortest distance between the center and the side of the square is 22 km. For accurate measurement of the distance, the geographical coordinates are projected into a two-dimensional coordinate system that preserves the distance with minimal distortion. The UTM grid system is used to determine the applicable projection for any given point taken from ESRI Data and Maps (2018).

Special consideration was taken for the Port of Rotterdam and the Port of Shanghai because the entirety of the port terminal extends beyond the 22 km boundary. For these cases, multiple port locations were used representing various terminal locations spread across the port. The corresponding AOI is the combination of the square boundaries of the terminals. Figure 4.3 shows the distance-based AOIs for select ports of varying sizes. Note that the Yangshan terminal is separated from the Port of Shanghai.

Figure 4.3: Distance-Based Areas of Interest for Ports

a. Port of Colombo

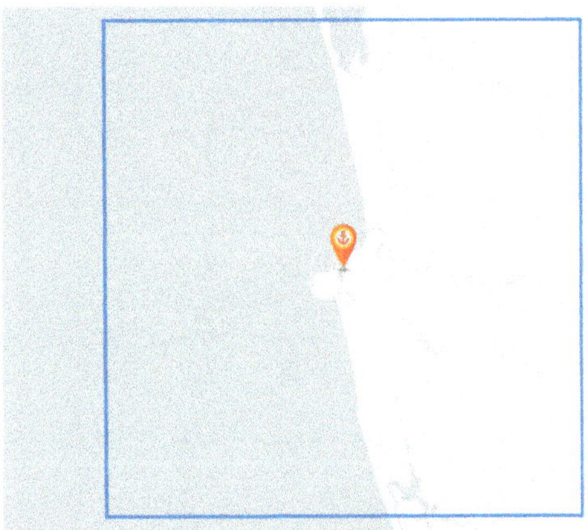

b. Port of Nuku'alofa

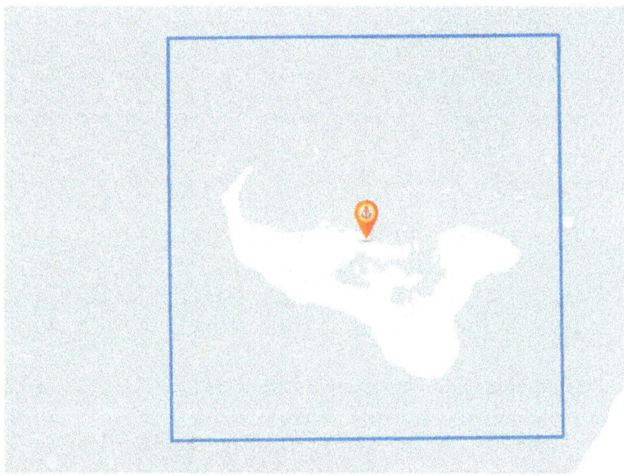

c. Port of Shanghai

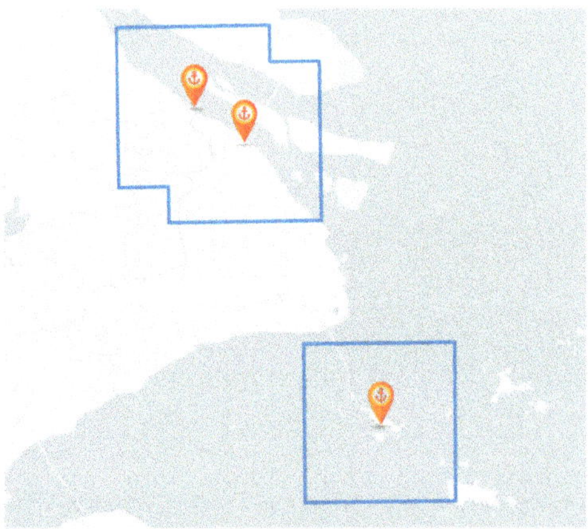

d. Port of Rotterdam

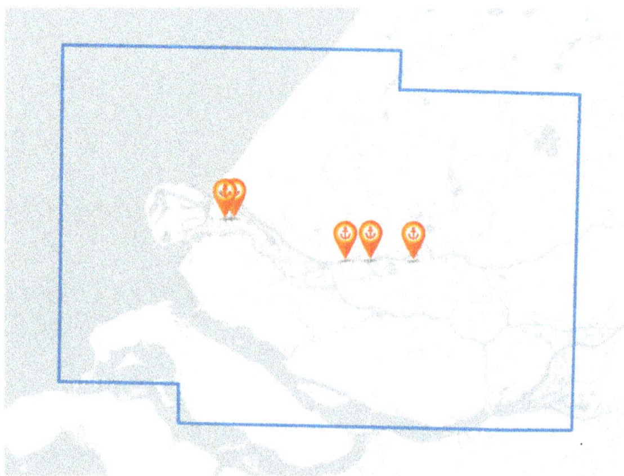

Note: Images are not proportional across maps.
Sources: Asian Development Bank calculations using National Geospatial-Intelligence Agency. 2020. World Port Index (Pub 150) Database. https://msi.nga.mil/Publications/WPI (accessed 21 June 2023); and ESRI Data and Maps. 2018. World UTM Grid Dataset. https://hub.arcgis.com/datasets/esri::world-utm-grid/ (accessed 21 June 2023).

Click here for figure data.

A sample of the python implementation to generate the AOIs given a set of port points is provided in Python Script 4.3. Note that the coordinate system that uses longitude and latitude pairs is 4326. The chosen projection is 3238 which converts the geolocation into units of meters.

Python Script 4.3: Generating Distance-Based Area of Interest

Script

```
1   import geopandas as gpd
2   import pandas as pd
3
4   df = pd.read_csv('port_long_lat.csv')
5   gdf = gpd.GeoDataFrame(df, crs=4326,
6       geometry=gpd.GeoSeries.from_xy(df['longitude'], df['latitude']))
7   gdf['AOI_projected'] = gdf.to_crs(3232).buffer(22000, cap_style=3)
8   gdf.set_geometry('AOI_projected', inplace=True)
9   gdf['AOI'] = gdf['AOI_projected'].to_crs('epsg:4326')
10  gdf.set_geometry('AOI', inplace=True)
```

Description

Lines	Description
1–2	Import necessary libraries.
4	Read the csv file containing the latitude and longitude per port as a pandas dataframe.
5–6	Convert the pandas dataframe to geopandas dataframe, with base crs 4326 and geometry the longitude and latitude pairs.
7	Project the geometry to 3232, and then generate the square boundary with distance 22,000 meters.
8–9	Project the geometry back to 4326 and set as AOI.

Source: Asian Development Bank.

4.2.3 Cluster-based Area of Interest

The cluster-based approach uses an algorithm to identify the clustering of a given AIS message. The 22 km distance-based AOI is used as the base area to apply the algorithm. Pedregosa et al. (2011) provide a comparison of the various algorithms in identifying clusters using generated datasets of varying shapes. Among the algorithms, only those that were based on the density of the clusters can accurately identify the grouping for datasets with irregular shapes and, by design, separate the noise from the data. The most popular of density-based algorithm is Density Based Spatial Clustering Algorithm with Noise (DBSCAN) which views clusters as areas of high density separated by low density clusters.[6] Considering these factors, DBSCAN is the chosen algorithm for the cluster-based approach. Its ability to handle clusters of varying shapes, consider density information, and identify outliers makes it well-suited for accurately identifying AOIs.

6 In addition, Hierarchical DBSCAN (HDBSCAN) and Ordering Points to Identify Clustering Structure (OPTICS) represent suitable algorithms since they are able to detect clusters with varying density (and allow for tuning of parameters). However, HDBSCAN and OPTICS involve relatively high computational complexity and power.

The DBSCAN algorithm works by grouping location points that are at least a minimum number of location points, called MinPts, within epsilon (∈) distance from each other (Ester, et al. 1996). Epsilon (∈) affects the granularity of the clusters while MinPts affects the size of the clusters and the sensitivity of the algorithm to outliers. The two parameters, ∈ and MinPts are user-defined.

Figure 4.4 provides a graphical representation of the workings of DBSCAN. The circles represent a set of location points that are within ∈ distance from each other. The three circles containing blue points have at least four location points each and share some location points. Setting MinPts to four, groups together all the blue points into one cluster. On the other hand, the orange points do not contain the minimum required location point and therefore are considered noise. If MinPts is set to 2, then the orange points will form another cluster. Note that they are not combined with the blue points because none of the orange points are within ∈ distance from the blue points. If ∈ is increased to the distance between the nearest blue point and orange point, then all the points will form a cluster. The choice of ∈ and MinPts is an important factor in determining the performance of the algorithm. These should be carefully considered based on the characteristics of the dataset and desired outcomes.

Figure 4.4: Graphical Representation of the Density-Based Spatial Clustering of Applications with Noise (DBSCAN) Algorithm

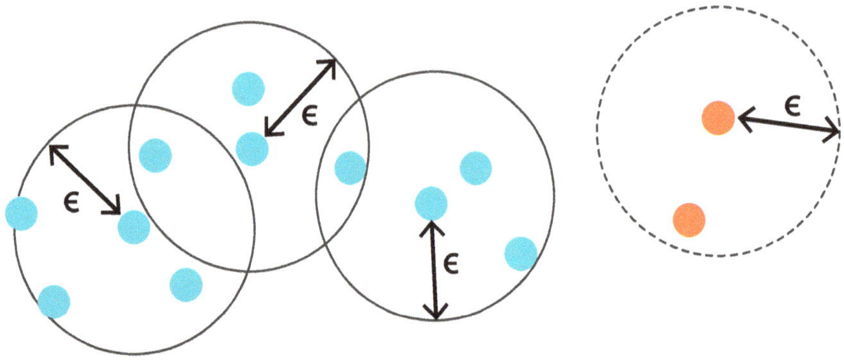

Notes: Each circle represents a location point. Blue points are grouped while orange points are considered noise. Parameters used are ∈ and 4 for minimum points.
Source: M. Ester, et al. 1996. A density-based algorithm for discovering clusters in large spatial databases with noise. *Knowledge Discovery and Data Mining* vol. 96, pp. 226–231.

Click here for figure data.

DBSCAN requires the calculation of all possible pairs of location points to determine the distance. While there are techniques to reduce the number of calculations required, the time complexity, and resource requirements increase with the number of location points, a huge challenge especially with big data. However, there is yet no application of DBSCAN specifically for big data. With the amount of AIS data transmitted in AOIs, performing DBSCAN on all location points is not practical. To address this, the H3 index is used to aggregate the location points, and as basis for inputs to the DBSCAN parameters.

H3 indices as location points in DBSCAN

Depending on the level of accuracy of the required clusters, some variation in location points is permissible as long as it does not influence the model results. For example, if the desired clustering threshold is within 500 m, a difference of 10 m would not have a significant impact on the clustering outcome. Note that the higher the resolution, the finer the clusters will be. However, this will come at the expense of higher model complexity as the number of indices increases. Hence, we recommend the use of a high resolution H3 with a manageable number of unique indices to represent the location points. H3 resolution 8 has an average edge length of 461 m which is about the length of longest ship ever constructed. The 22 km square boundary contains approximately 1,000 unique indices. Increasing the resolution by 1 reduces the average H3 edge length to 200 m. However, the number of unique indices for the same square boundary is increased to 4,000. Using a higher resolution of 12 increases the number of unique indices to about 93,000, but results in a very fine average edge length of around 10 m. Figure 4.5 shows the difference in sizes for both resolutions overlayed on a port terminal.

For DBSCAN, the centers of the hexagons will be the location points and the frequency of AIS messages will be the weight of the location point. This aggregation of location points can lead to a significant decline in the complexity of the model without losing much accuracy in the clusters.

Figure 4.5: Choropleth Map of Automatic Identification System Message Density per Select H3 Resolutions for the Port of Odesa

a. Resolution 8 | b. Resolution 9 | c. Resolution 12

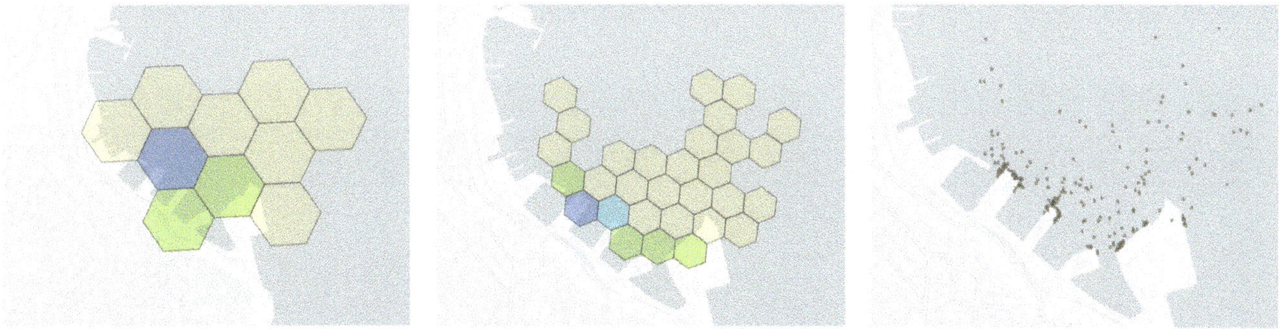

Note: The darker the color, the more AIS messages it contains.
Sources: Asian Development Bank calculations using United Nations Global Platform for Official Statistics. 2023. AIS Data. https://officialstatistics.org/ (accessed 31 August 2023); Uber Technologies. 2023. H3 version 3. https://h3geo.org/; Maps are generated using V. Agafonkin, et al. 2023. Leaflet / Leaflet v.1.9.4. https://leafletjs.com/; OpenStreetMap. https://www.openstreetmap.org/copyright.; and Carto. https://carto.com/attribution/.

Click here for figure data.

H3 frequency as Basis for DBSCAN Parameters

In Figure 4.6, the Choropleth map shows the high-density areas. In a way, it shows potential clusters with varying level of sizes. The H3 resolution acts as the ϵ distance and the frequency of the index as MinPts, where an H3 index must have a minimum number of points to be included in the cluster. These provide a basis for potential values of DBSCAN parameters.

The choice for ϵ is straightforward. It is recommended to use the average edge length of the H3 resolution as the value. For the MinPts, it is recommended to use the frequency of the H3 index with the lowest number of location points but part of the top H3 indices that cover a high percentage of the frequency. To illustrate, given a boundary, get the H3 indices that contribute to the top xth percentile of the location points. From here, the number of location points in the H3 index with the lowest frequency will be the MinPts. Note that the higher the value of the percentile, the higher the MinPts, the larger the resulting clusters will be. However, the average sizes of the cluster are generally affected by the ϵ.

A sample implementation of this method is found in Python Script 4.4. Here, the location points used in the DBSCAN model are the center points of H3 index resolution 12. The center points are transformed to the appropriate projection of the area. To get the

Figure 4.6: Yearly Cluster-Based Area of Interest for Ports of Los Angeles and Long Beach

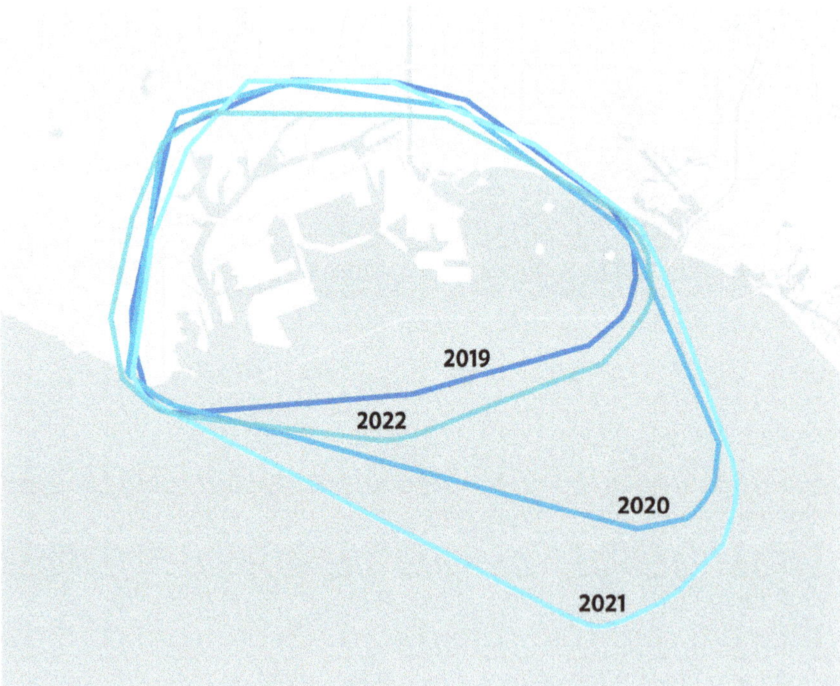

Sources: Asian Development Bank calculations using United Nations Global Platform for Official Statistics. 2023. AIS Data. https://officialstatistics.org/ (accessed 31 August 2023); Map is generated using V. Agafonkin, et al. 2023. Leaflet / Leaflet v.1.9.4. https://leafletjs.com/; OpenStreetMap. https://www.openstreetmap.org/copyright.; and Carto. https://carto.com/attribution/.

Click here for figure data.

Python Script 4.4: DBSCAN Modeling

Script

```
1   import h3.api.numpy_int as h3int
2   from sklearn.cluster import DBSCAN
3   from pyproj import Transformer
4
5   def get_parameters(df, cluster_res, per):
6       eps_m = round(h3int.edge_length(cluster_res) * 1000)
7       df[‘h3_cluster_index’] = df[‘H3_int_index_12’] \
8           .apply(lambda x: h3int.h3_to_parent(x, cluster_res))
9
10      df_cluster = df.groupby(‘h3_cluster_index’)[‘count_mmsi’].sum() \
11          .reset_index() \
12          .sort_values(‘count_mmsi’,ignore_index=True, ascending=False)
13      df_cluster[‘cumsum’] = df_cluster[‘count_mmsi’].cumsum()
14      tot = df_cluster.count_mmsi.sum()
15      df_cluster[‘cumper’] = df_cluster[‘cumsum’] / tot
16
17      min_points = df_cluster[df_cluster.cumper >= per].iloc[0].count_mmsi
18      return eps_m, int(min_points)
19
20  sdf_agg = aoi_naoi_sdf.filter(
21      (F.col(‘area’) == ‘aoi’) & (F.col(‘stationary’) == ‘Y’)) \
22      .groupBy(‘H3_int_index_12’) \
23      .agg(F.count(‘mmsi’).alias(‘count_mmsi’))
24
25  df = sdf_agg.toPandas()
26  eps_m, min_points = get_parameters(df,
27      cluster_res = 8,
28      per = 0.90)
29  model = DBSCAN(eps=eps_m,min_samples=min_points)
30
31  points = df[‘H3_int_index_12’].apply(lambda x: h3int.h3_to_geo(x))
32  df[‘latitude’], df[‘longitude’] = zip(*points)
33
34  transf = Transformer.from_crs(4326, epsg_to=3832, always_xy=True)
35  (df[‘long_t’], df[‘lat_t’]) = transf.transform(df[‘longitude’].values,
36                      df[‘latitude’].values)
37
38  X = df[[‘long_t’, ‘lat_t’]].values
39  sample_weight = df[‘count_mmsi’].values
40  model_fit = model.fit(X, sample_weight=sample_weight)
```

Description

1–3	Import necessary Python packages.
5–18	Create wrapper function to compute ∈ and MinPts given the H3 resolution and percentile.
20–23	From the aoi_naoi_sdf output of Python Script 4.1, get the count of AIS messages per H3_int_index_12.
25	Convert the sdf_agg output from spark dataframe to pandas dataframe.
26–29	Compute the DBSCAN parameters using H3 resolution 8 and percentile 0.90 and produce the model.
31–36	Get the central points of the H3 indices and transform to projection 3832.
38–40	Fit the DBSCAN model to the projected points.

Source: Asian Development Bank.

parameters, the H3 resolution 8 is used as basis for the ∈ distance and the 90th percentile is used to derive the MinPts. After the parameters are calculated, the DBSCAN model is fitted using the projected points and the parameters.

A set of different values for H3 resolutions and percentile cut-offs can be tested to see which parameters will arrive at the desired cluster. DBSCAN requires careful parameter tuning. This process often involves a combination of domain knowledge and trial and error to determine the optimal parameter values for a given dataset. MinPts can be treated with more flexibility as it has little impact on the results of the clusters in comparison to ∈ (Shubert, et al. 2017). The best model should be selected based on technical criteria and subjective preferences depending on the target of the analysis. This study's technical criteria are as follows: (i) a limited number of clusters, (ii) able to capture known areas of EOI (such as berths for ports), (iii) identification of noise since not all stops lead to true EOI, and iv) metric for quality of cluster, if possible. An example of the metric is Density-Based Clustering Validation (DBCV) index (Moulavi, et al. 2014) which assesses the clustering quality based on the within-and between- cluster density connectedness of clusters. However, DBCV requires more computation power than the cluster algorithm and therefore inefficient when applied to big data.

When a final cluster is selected, the H3 resolution and percentile corresponding to the cluster will be the final model parameters. It should be noted that even when the H3 resolution and percentile parameters are fixed, the resulting clusters may change with new data. This is because the corresponding ∈ and MinPts may change with events that may affect the distribution of the data, such as port expansions, and port congestion. These dynamic changes are automatically reflected when determining the DBSCAN parameters.

For analysis of ports over a long period of time, it is necessary to have a stable AOI definition. Thus, the data from the DBSCAN for the entire period in consideration should be used to establish the *reference* AOI. This is done by combining the results of the clusters from different periods to arrive at a single cluster that covers all the period specific AOIs. An example of this is for the ports of Los Angeles and Long Beach, where the AOIs generated for 2019 and 2022 were considerably smaller than the ones for 2020 and 2021 (Figure 4.6). The reference AOI is the polygon that encompasses all the year specific AOIs.

Figure 4.7 shows the cluster-based AOI for the selected ports and passageways. Note that for the Port of Shanghai, the boundary is not contiguous, with the larger AOI comprising the primary terminals of Wusongku and Waigaoquiao and the smaller AOI comprising the Yangshan terminal. The calculations obtained for each AOI are then summed up to get the indicators for the Port of Shanghai.

Figure 4.7: Cluster-Based Areas of Interest

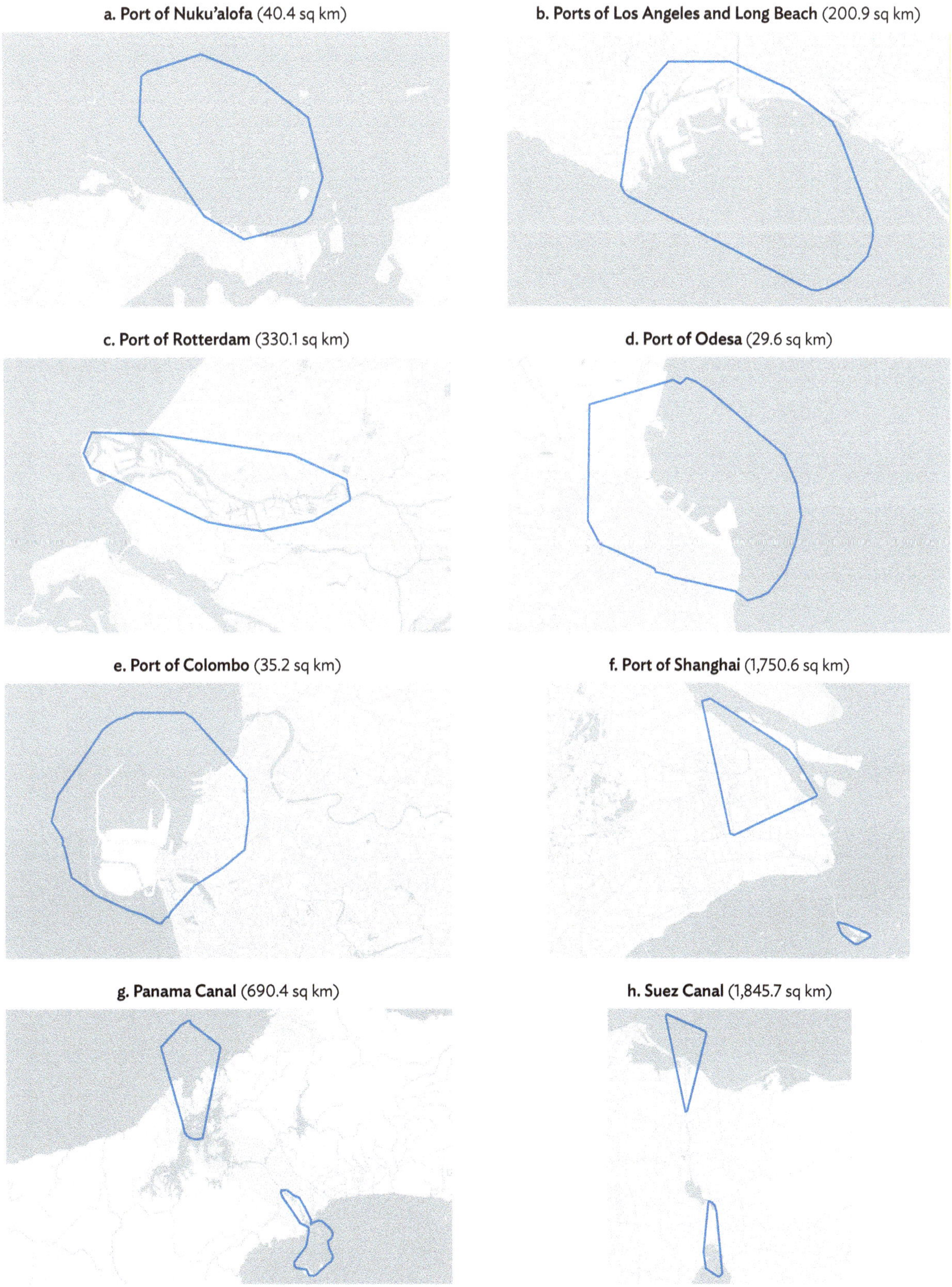

sq km = square kilometer

Notes: Images are not proportional across maps. The areas are computed by automatically from geojson.io.

Sources: Asian Development Bank calculations using United Nations Global Platform for Official Statistics. 2023. AIS Data. https://officialstatistics.org/ (accessed 31 August 2023); Map is generated using V. Agafonkin, et al. 2023. Leaflet / Leaflet v.1.9.4. https://leafletjs.com/; OpenStreetMap. https://www.openstreetmap.org/copyright.; and Carto. https://carto.com/attribution/.

Click here for figure data.

4.3 Generation of Indicators

Reviewing Data Quality

To check data quality, the daily counts of unique vessels were computed for all AOIs. The resulting time series were compared to known dates with data quality issues identified from section 2.3, particularly low count of AIS messages, spoofing and anomalies. It was observed that the dates identified to have the lowest count of AIS messages (12 May 2022 and 14 February 2023) also produced a low count of unique vessels in the AOIs. This is regardless of the AOI location or size. For these dates, the data is assumed incomplete, thus corresponding indicators are treated as missing for the day.

For spoofing or anomalies which occurred from 27 January–2 February 2020, there were spikes in the daily counts of unique vessels for all port AOIs, but not for passageway AOIs. Figure 4.8 shows the counts of unique vessels for port AOIs in 2020, standardized for comparison across AOIs. The dates when the spikes occurred were the same across all AOIs, including the Port of Shanghai which saw a general decrease in counts in early 2020. It was inferred that the spikes resulted due to the large number of MMSIs that appeared to be in the AOIs yet sent only one signal within the day, which is unlikely given the characteristics of the vessels. When these vessels were removed from the analysis (either by checking the number of messages sent per vessel or the time spent in the AOIs within the day), the issues seem to disappear.

The implementation of the data quality processing steps in Python varies per indicator. Thus, the corresponding script for data cleaning is included in the Python script to generate each indicator.

Figure 4.8: Standardized Daily Count of Unique Vessels for Ports, 2020

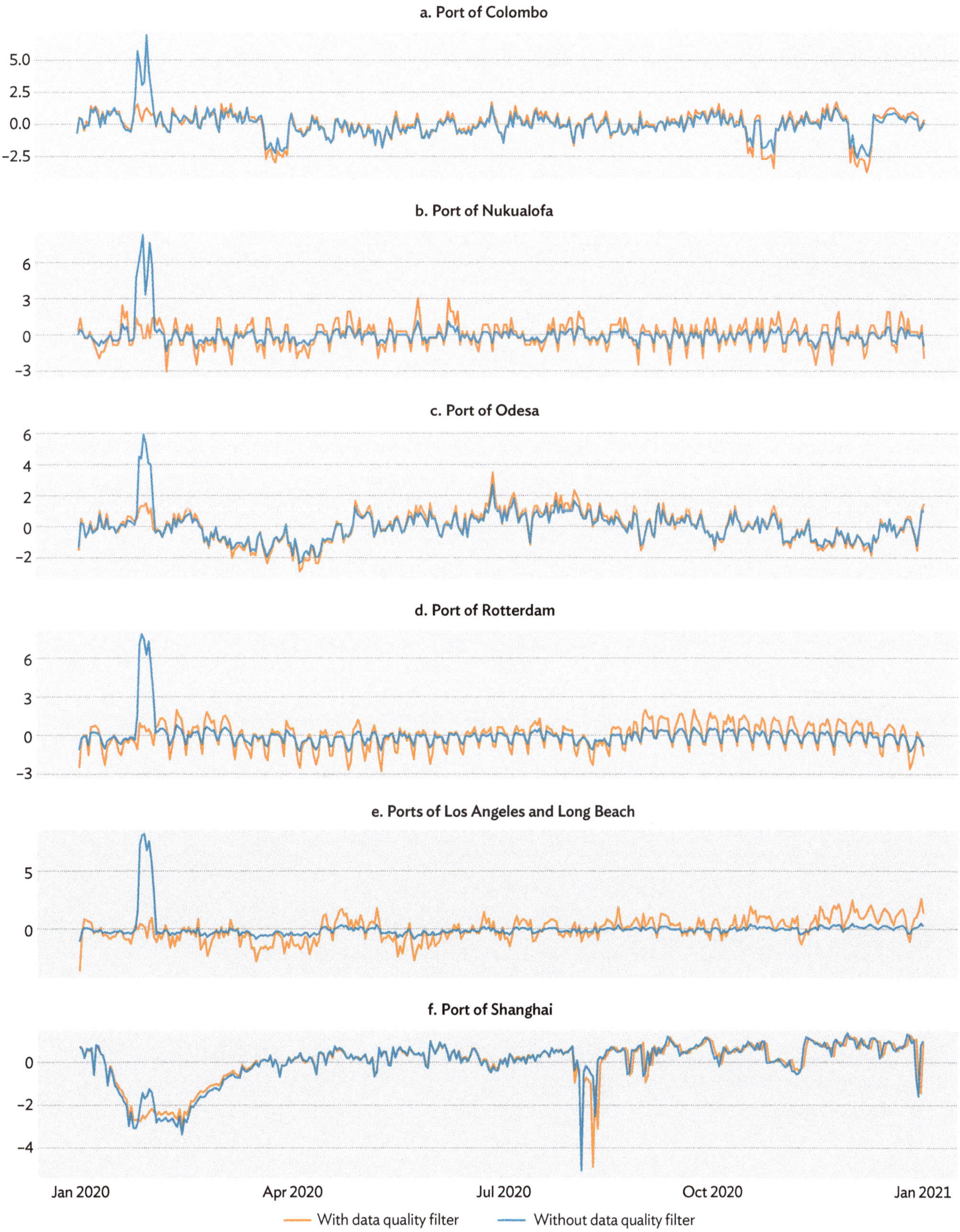

Source: Asian Development Bank calculations using United Nations Global Platform for Official Statistics. 2023. AIS Data. https://officialstatistics.org/ (accessed 31 August 2023).

Click here for figure data.

Count of Unique Vessels

The daily counts of unique vessels were generated using cluster-based AOIs for ports and manual AOIs for passageways. From the data preparation steps, AIS messages from individual vessels that are within the AOIs and non-AOIs were retrieved. The data is further filtered by getting the messages that are only within the AOIs. To apply the data quality processing steps, the count of AIS messages, minimum SOG, minimum datetime, and maximum datetime was computed per MMSI per day. Only vessels that made a stop, sent at least two AIS messages at different times within the day were retained. The count of unique MMSIs retained per day became the indicator. Python Script 4.6 shows the implementation of this.

Python Script 4.6: Computing Count of Unique Vessels Indicator

Script

```
1   aoi_sdf = aoi_naoi_sdf.filter(F.col(‘area’)==’aoi’) \
2     .withColumn(‘date’, F.to_date(‘dt_pos_utc’)) \
3     .groupBy(‘date’,’mmsi’).agg(F.count(F.lit(1)).alias(‘count_ais’),
4                       F.min(‘sog’).alias(‘min_sog’),
5                       F.min(‘dt_pos_utc’).alias(‘min_time’),
6                       F.max(‘dt_pos_utc’).alias(‘max_time’),
7                       ) \
8     .withColumn(‘time_spent_seconds’,
9       F.col(‘max_time’).cast(‘long’)
10      - F.col(‘min_time’).cast(‘long’)) \
11    .withColumn(‘time_spent_hours’,
12            F.col(‘time_spent_seconds’) / 3600)
13
14  daily_unique_count_indicator = aoi_sdf \
15    .filter((F.col(‘min_sog’) < 1) &
16         (F.col(‘time_spent_hours’) > 0) &
17         (F.col(‘count_ais’) > 1)) \
18    .groupBy(‘date’).agg(F.countDistinct(‘mmsi’).alias(‘count_vessel’))
```

Description

Line	Description
1	From the aoi_naoi_sdf output of Python Script 4.1, select only messages within AOI.
2–7	Create the date column and then per date and MMSI, get the count of AIS messages, minimum SOG, minimum and maximum time of position.
8–12	Compute the total time spent per day per MMSI in hours.
14–17	Get only MMSI that have stopped in the AOI, spent more than 0 hours, and sent at least 2 signals.
18	Compute the daily count of unique MMSI.

Source: Asian Development Bank.

Daily Arrivals and Median Time Spent in Ports

For port daily arrivals, the process is similar as before except that the aggregation is by MMSI and movement. The same aggregated columns are also computed, but with minimum datetime as the arrival date and maximum datetime as the departure date. The sample implementation is provided in Python Script 4.7.

Python Script 4.7: Computing the Daily Arrivals and Median Time Spent in Ports

Script

```
1   aoi_sdf = movement_flag_sdf.filter(F.col(‘area’)==’aoi’) \
2     .groupBy(‘mmsi’, ‘movement_group’).agg(F.count(F.lit(1)).alias(‘count_ais’),
3                          F.min(‘sog’).alias(‘min_sog’),
4                          F.min(‘dt_pos_utc’).alias(‘arrival_date’),
5                          F.max(‘dt_pos_utc’).alias(‘departure_date’),
6                         )\
7     .withColumn(‘time_spent_seconds’,
8       F.col(‘departure_date’).cast(‘long’)
9       - F.col(‘arrival_date’).cast(‘long’)) \
10    .withColumn(‘time_spent_hours’,
11            F.col(‘time_spent_seconds’) / 3600)
12
13  arrival_median_time_indicator = aoi_sdf \
14    .filter((F.col(‘min_sog’) < 1) &
15          (F.col(‘time_spent_hours’) > 0) &
16          (F.col(‘count_ais’) > 1)) \
17    .groupBy(‘arrival_date’).agg(F.count(F.lit(1)).alias(‘count_arrival’),
18                          F.percentile_approx(‘time_spent_hours’, 0.5) \
19                              .alias(‘median_time_spent’))
```

Description

1	From the movement_flag_sdf output of Python Script 4.1, select only messages that occurred within the AOI.
2–6	Get the count of AIS messages, minimum SOG, minimum date, and maximum date per MMSI per movement. The minimum and maximum dates represent the arrival and departure dates, respectively.
7–11	Compute the total time spent per movement per MMSI in hours.
13–16	Get only movements where the vessels made a stop in the AOI, spent more than 0 hours, and sent at least 2 signals.
17–19	Compute the count of the number of vessel arrivals and the median time spent per arrival day.

Source: Asian Development Bank.

Aggregate International Port Arrivals

For this indicator, the data preparation steps were applied to the entirety of the AIS data using the distance-based AOIs for all ports. This resulted in two derived data, Global Movements data and Port Calls data. The former is the aggregation of AIS data by vessel, by movement in and out of the AOIs, and by whether the vessel is stationary or not. The latter collects movements that are likely port calls. A detailed discussion of the derivation of the data is provided in the Appendix. From the Port Calls data, vessels that made port calls in at least two economies within the year were treated as vessels having international voyages. Moreover, only cargo, tanker, and passenger vessels are considered, the first two to represent commercial trade activity and the last to represent tourism.

Passageway Transits and Median Transit Time

For passageway transits, the movement to be tracked is not just an entry to and exit from a single AOI. The vessel must enter the passageway via one opening and exit through another. Therefore, when aggregating the movements, the first and last sub-areas which refer to the openings, where messages are located, must be marked. A transit is where the movement is in the AOI, and the first and last sub-areas are different. The sample implementation is provided in Python Script 4.8.

Python Script 4.8: Computing the Daily Arrivals and Median Time Spent in Passageways

Script

```
1   aoi_sdf = movement_flag_sdf.filter(F.col('area')=='aoi') \
2     .groupBy('mmsi','movement_group').agg(F.count(F.lit(1)).alias('count_ais'),
3               F.min('sog').alias('min_sog'),
4               F.min('dt_pos_utc').alias('arrival_date'),
5               F.max('dt_pos_utc').alias('departure_date'),
6               F.min_by('dt_pos_utc','sub_area').alias('arrival_sub_area'),
7               F.max_by('dt_pos_utc','sub_area').alias('departure_sub_area')
8                    ) \
9     .withColumn('time_spent_seconds',
10        F.col('departure_date').cast('long')
11        - F.col('arrival_date').cast('long')) \
12    .withColumn('time_spent_hours',
13             F.col('time_spent_seconds') / 3600)
14
15  arrival_median_time_indicator = aoi_sdf \
16    .filter((F.col('min_sog') < 1) &
17         (F.col('time_spent_hours') > 0) &
18         (F.col('count_ais') > 1) &
19         (F.col('arrival_sub_area') != F.col('departure_sub_area')) ) \
20    .groupBy('arrival_date').agg(F.count(F.lit(1)).alias('count_arrival'),
21                   F.percentile_approx('time_spent_hours', 0.5) \
22                      .alias('median_transit_time'))
```

Description	
1	From the movement_flag_sdf output of Python Script 4.1 with changes applied from Python Script 4.2, select only messages that occurred within AOI.
2–8	Get the count of AIS messages, minimum SOG, minimum date, and maximum date, opening sub area on minimum date, and opening sub area on maximum date per MMSI per movement. The minimum and maximum dates represent the arrival and departure dates, respectively.
7–11	Compute the total time spent per movement per MMSI in hours.
15–19	Get only movements where the vessels made a stop in the AOI, spent more than 0 hours, and sent at least 2 signals, and the arrival sub area is different from the departure sub area. The last criteria ensures that the vessel moved from one opening to the other and therefore made a transit.
20–22	Compute the count of the number of vessel arrivals and the median transit_time per arrival day.

Source: Asian Development Bank.

Chapter 5

Automatic Identification System Indicators for Maritime Hubs

While Chapters 3 and 4 detail the formulation of concepts, definitions, and indicators for developing a framework for discerning the state and evolution of maritime transportation and port operations from AIS data, Chapters 5 and 6 demonstrate how the framework can be used to examine real world activity. This chapter focuses on applications to major maritime hubs using the AIS data generated since 2019, and statistics are analyzed from both global and regional perspectives. In particular, it explores trends in East Asia, Europe, the Americas, and the Middle East. The COVID-19 pandemic and the Russian invasion of Ukraine wrought pervasive economic consequences during the period covered. While both events had significant effects on the global economy, findings suggest that maritime activity withstood these shocks remarkably.

5.1 Aggregate International Port Arrivals

To provide a macro-level view of maritime activity, this section presents port statistics derived from AIS data aggregated to the global level. Port locations were obtained from the World Port Index, and daily counts of vessels (as defined in section 3.1.2) were calculated for each and then summed. Because of the large number of ports (> 3,700), only the distance-based approach to defining the area of interest (AOI) was feasible.[7] The UNCLOS territorial limit of 22 km was used. For a vessel to be counted, it should have made an international voyage, here defined as having made a port visit in at least two economies within the year. Moreover, only cargo, tanker, and passenger vessels are considered to signify potential signals of economic activity—the first two taken to represent commercial trade and the last to represent tourism.

Figure 5.1 presents the daily counts of international port arrivals, with subdivisions for cargo, tanker, and passenger vessels. Arrivals spiked in December 2019 and early January 2020. The spike occurred around the time the People's Republic of China (PRC) first imposed lockdowns in Hubei Province following the outbreak of the COVID-19 pandemic—implying that while this could have been a measurement error, it might have been driven by actual phenomena. This period does not coincide with that related to the spoofing activity which affected all ports, an issue already addressed through the specific methods detailed in this study.[8] A similar trend is seen specifically in the Port of Shanghai (Figure 5.4) but not in the other ports studied (Figures 5.8, 5.9). Future studies are necessary for a deeper understanding of such anomalies.

7 See section 3.1.1 for the advantages and disadvantages of this approach.

8 See section 4.3.

Figure 5.1: Daily Count of International Port Arrivals by Category, 2019–2023

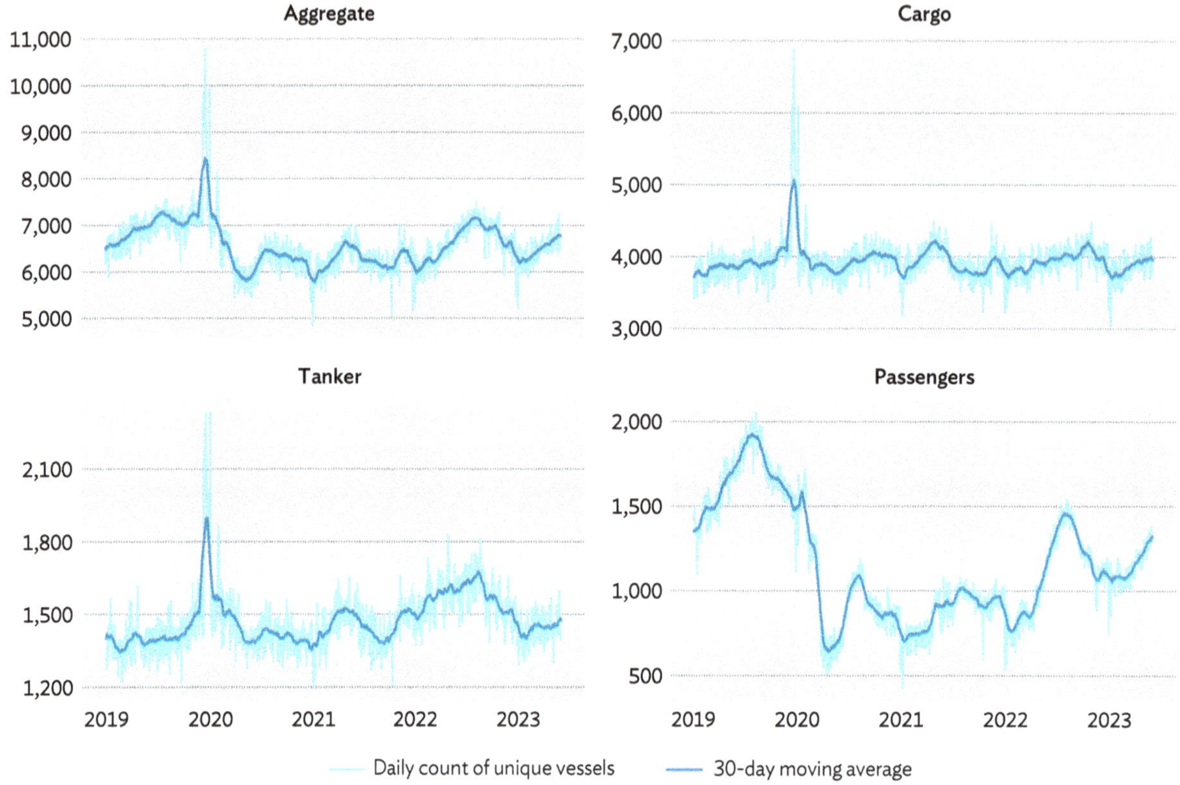

Note: Figures exclude the start and end of the period (1 January 2019; 31 May 2023) and dates affected by data quality issues (29 April–1 May 2019; 12–3 May 2022; 14–15 February 2023).
Sources: Asian Development Bank calculations using United Nations Global Platform for Official Statistics. 2023. AIS Data and Ship Registry Dataset. https://officialstatistics.org/ (accessed 31 August 2023); and National Geospatial-Intelligence Agency. 2020. World Port Index (Pub 150) Database. https://msi.nga.mil/Publications/WPI (accessed 21 June 2023).

Click here for figure data.

The lockdown measures pursued by much of the world throughout 2020 and 2021 manifested in lower international port arrivals in the aggregate. This drop appears to have been driven mainly by passenger vessels, which saw daily port visits fall from over 1500 to about 600. The spike is not present in the passenger vessels data, which makes the drop all the more dramatic. Cargo and tanker visits, meanwhile, actually held steady at about their 2019 levels. This demonstrates the highly unusual nature of the pandemic-induced economic downturn in that consumer demand was frustrated but not destroyed. As purchases shifted online, goods still needed to be shipped across maritime highways, necessitating the continued port visits of cargo ships.

Whereas the pandemic did not significantly affect tanker visits, the Russian invasion of Ukraine in February 2022 had a profound impact on this indicator. Figure 5.1 shows elevated levels of port arrivals in the period coinciding with the invasion. The global trade in energy commodities, particularly oil, experienced massive volatility in the months after the invasion, with sanctions on the Russian Federation forcing the hasty rerouting of oil deliveries across the world. This period of adjustment may have caused the increase seen in port visits. This is supported by the fact that arrivals returned to baseline levels when oil prices subsided in the latter half of 2022.

To tease out finer trends, data for vessel subcategories are plotted in Figure 5.2. The fall in cruise ship arrivals was more pronounced than the overall fall in passenger vessel arrivals, dropping from 150–200 a day to a low of less than 20 a day at the onset of the pandemic. This is to be expected as cruises are a non-essential service with enclosed spaces that make them prime targets for pandemic restrictions. Their recovery, however, was nearly as rapid, having been back to pre-pandemic levels since 2022. On the other hand, recovery in roll-on/roll-off (RORO) passenger ship arrivals have not been as complete, remaining at around 750 arrivals a day compared with almost 1,000 in 2019. This might suggest a sustained decrease in the demand for non-recreational travel as online means of communication became more accepted during the pandemic.

Figure 5.2: Daily Count of International Port Arrivals by Subcategory, 2019–2023

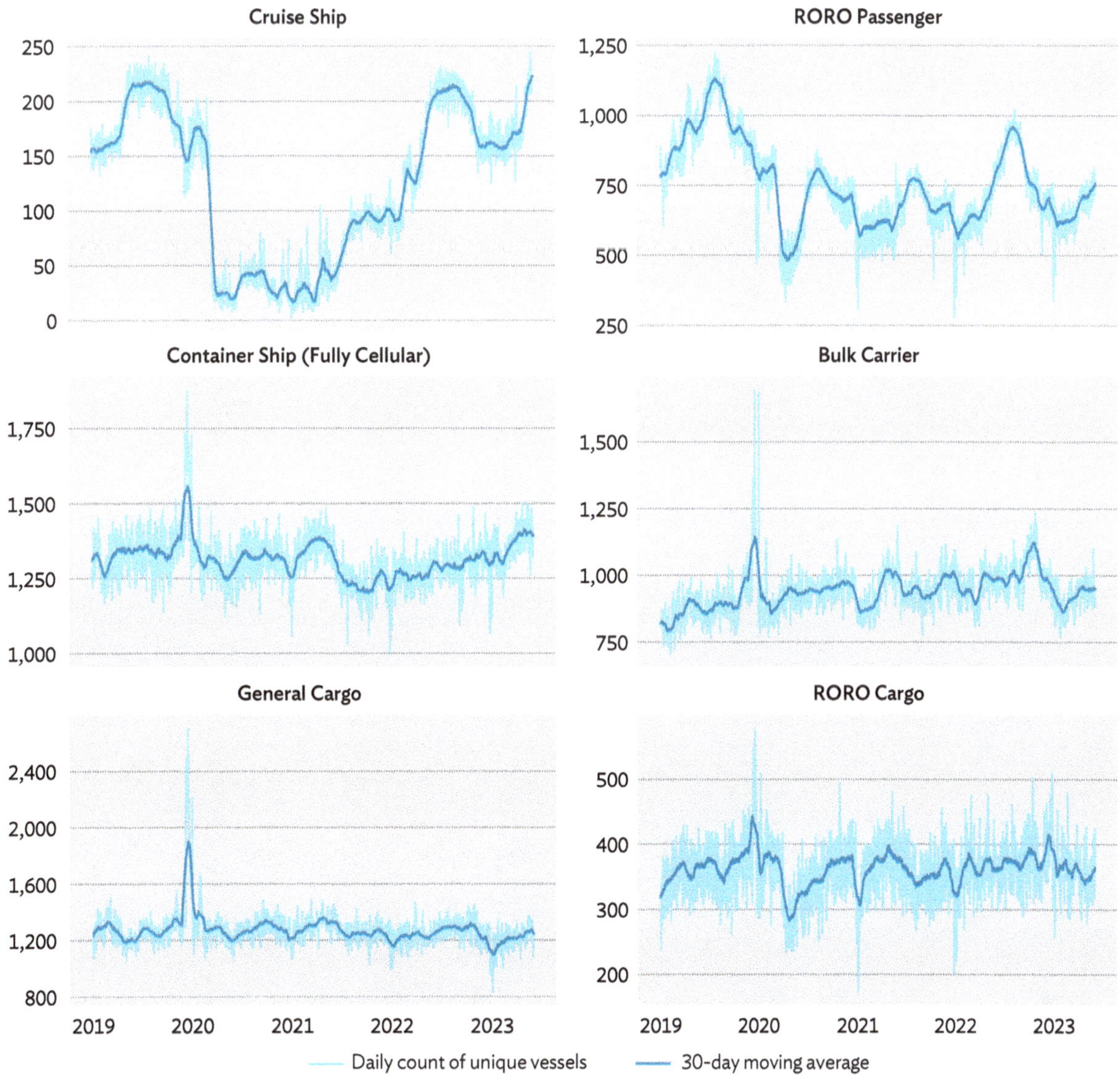

RORO = roll-on/roll-off.

Note: Figures exclude the start and end of the period (1 January 2019; 31 May 2023) and dates affected by data quality issues (29 April–1 May 2019; 12–13 May 2022; 14–15 February 2023).

Sources: Asian Development Bank calculations using United Nations Global Platform for Official Statistics. 2023. AIS Data and Ship Registry Dataset. https://officialstatistics.org/ (accessed 31 August 2023); and National Geospatial-Intelligence Agency. 2020. World Port Index (Pub 150) Database. https://msi.nga.mil/Publications/WPI (accessed 21 June 2023).

Click here for figure data.

Mirroring the trends in overall cargo arrivals are the arrivals in subcategories of cargo vessels. The steadiest are general cargo ships, whose arrivals (apart from the early 2020 spike) have stayed at around 1200–1300 a day for all the years in the plot. Container ships, bulk carriers, and RORO ships are more variable but have generally also maintained a consistent level. Overall, maritime trade appears to have remained remarkably resilient even in the face of the COVID-19 pandemic and the Russian invasion of Ukraine, a testament to the robustness of the global maritime economy.

5.2 Regional

While the aggregate indicators provide a bird's-eye view of global activity, region-specific trends may be examined by deriving indicators for select ports and passageways. This portion examines East Asia, Europe, the Americas, and the Middle East (Table 3.2). Given the smaller collection of ports under consideration, the cluster-based approach to defining the AOI is used throughout. Note that seasonality is evident in many of the series plotted, suggesting that some form of seasonal adjustment may be desirable depending on the research question.

5.2.1 East Asia

East Asia is represented in this section by the Port of Shanghai—the world's largest and busiest port—and the straits of Malacca and Singapore, which connect the region to the west. East Asia is the home of the second- and third-largest economies in the world, the PRC and Japan, as well as the high-income economies of the Republic of Korea, and Taipei,China. It is also economically well connected to the Association of Southeast Asian Nations, a major trading bloc. Trends in its maritime activity can therefore be of global consequence.

The Port of Shanghai, depicted in Figure 5.3, handles over 25% of all trade carried out in the PRC and approximately 99% of Shanghai's foreign trade activities. The port's strategic location gives it a vital advantage, with its connection to the Yangtze River

Figure 5.3: The Port of Shanghai

Source: Shanghai International Port (Group) Co., Ltd. Port of Shanghai image. https://en.portshanghai.com.cn/r/cms/www/emobile/images/slider/layer/slide1-bg.jpg (accessed 26 June 2023).

Click here for figure data.

allowing it to serve as a gateway to inland provinces. The Port of Shanghai has three main terminals: Wusongku, Waigaoqiao, and Yangshan. The last was developed only in 2005 due to insufficient water depth in the port's terminal.

Panel (a) of Figure 5.4 depicts the daily count of unique vessels in the Port of Shanghai from January 2019 to May 2023. Throughout the period covered, this count fluctuated around the 3000 mark, with significant peaks and dips. Vessel counts plunged at the start of 2020 as the PRC began locking down areas in Hubei Province, the site of the first recorded COVID-19 outbreak. This coincides with the spike in global arrivals seen in Figure 5.1. How the two are related remains unclear and is left for future work, but be it a dip or a spike, the abrupt turn in the indicator is suggestive of unusual activity. Another lockdown-associated drop was seen in April to May of 2022, when the city of Shanghai was locked down due to a COVID-19 outbreak. It is worth noting that while the indicators began rebounding even before the Hubei lockdowns ended, they remained depressed all throughout the Shanghai lockdowns. This suggests that the Port of Shanghai remained resilient during the Hubei lockdowns, but shutdowns in the city of Shanghai itself caused more persistent dislocations in the port. Interestingly, however, it appears that shipping had grown more adaptable to such scenarios as the fall in vessel counts in 2022 was not as deep as that of 2020.

Other outliers in the indicator appear to have had a technical root. For instance, the marked increase in vessel counts seen from November to December 2021 could be attributed to changes in AIS data gathering following the AIS blackout in the PRC for a few days after the passage of the Personal Protection Information Law on 1 November 2022 (Olcott, Dempsey and Bernard 2021). However, the drivers of other significant movements are less clear. There appears to be a recurring seasonal drop close to the start of each year (with the drop in 2020 amplified by the lockdowns). This study has not been able to establish the precise causes of such occurrences.

The vessel counts and the median hours spent in port are depicted in panels (b) and (c), respectively, of Figure 5.4. Note that the highest spike in panel (b) and the lowest drop in panel (c) occurred during the same period when international port arrivals spiked (Figure 5.1)—prior the Hubei lockdowns. Further investigation shows that the average number of daily port arrivals per vessel during this period increased from 1 to 4. This anomaly is caused by some vessels registering daily arrivals as high as 100, spending only a few minutes per visit. As a result, the median time spent in a port was drastically reduced. Thus, the dates affected by this aberration are excluded from the analysis. For the periods not affected by this issue, the trends in vessel counts are consistent with those related to vessel arrivals and median hours spent in port.

Figure 5.4: Port Activity Indicators, Port of Shanghai, 2019–2023

Notes:
1. Figures exclude dates affected by data quality issues (12 May 2022; 14 February 2023), and the start and end of the period (1 January 2019; 31 May 2023) for panels b and c.
2. Hubei lockdown: 23 January–8 April 2020.
3. Russian invasion of Ukraine: 24 February 2022.
4. Shanghai lockdown: 1 April–1 June 2022.

Source: Asian Development Bank calculations using United Nations Global Platform for Official Statistics. 2023. AIS Data. https://officialstatistics.org/ (accessed 31 August 2023).

Click here for figure data.

To provide a better sense of long-run trends, Table 5.1 shows averages per year for the indicators discussed above. All three decreased only modestly in 2020 compared to 2019, a testament to the relatively successful management of the pandemic in the PRC during this time. By 2021, the counts of unique vessels and vessel arrivals have surpassed their 2019 levels. This also resulted in higher median hours spent from 33 in 2019 to 35 in 2021. However, it was in 2022 when the PRC experienced a more challenging COVID-19 environment, necessitating, among other measures, lockdowns in Shanghai. Vessel counts in the Port of Shanghai on an average day fell from 3,219 to 3,067; arrivals, meanwhile, fell from 451 vessels to 395, lower even than 2019.

Table 5.1: Yearly Average of Daily Indicators, Port of Shanghai, 2019–2022

	Count of Unique Vessels	Vessel Arrivals	Median Hours Spent
2019	2,945	407	33
2020	2,912	398	32
2021	3,219	451	35
2022	3,067	395	32

Note: For vessel arrivals and median hours spent, the indicators during the identified data quality issue are not included (10 December 2019–2 January 2020).
Source: Asian Development Bank calculations using United Nations Global Platform for Official Statistics. 2023. AIS Data. https://officialstatistics.org/ (accessed 31 August 2023).

Figure 5.5 presents another annual summary of port activity in Shanghai. In this plot, the yearly number of arrivals by vessel category is depicted as indexed to 2019 levels. The chart reiterates the observation made above that merchant ships were less affected by lockdowns than non-merchant and passenger ships. Indeed, arrivals from the latter two in 2022 saw the most significant drop from the 2019 levels. On the other hand, fishing vessels continually increased, with the highest in 2022, despite the multiple lockdowns.

Figure 5.5: Yearly Vessel Arrivals by Category, Port of Shanghai, 2020–2022
(2019 = 100)

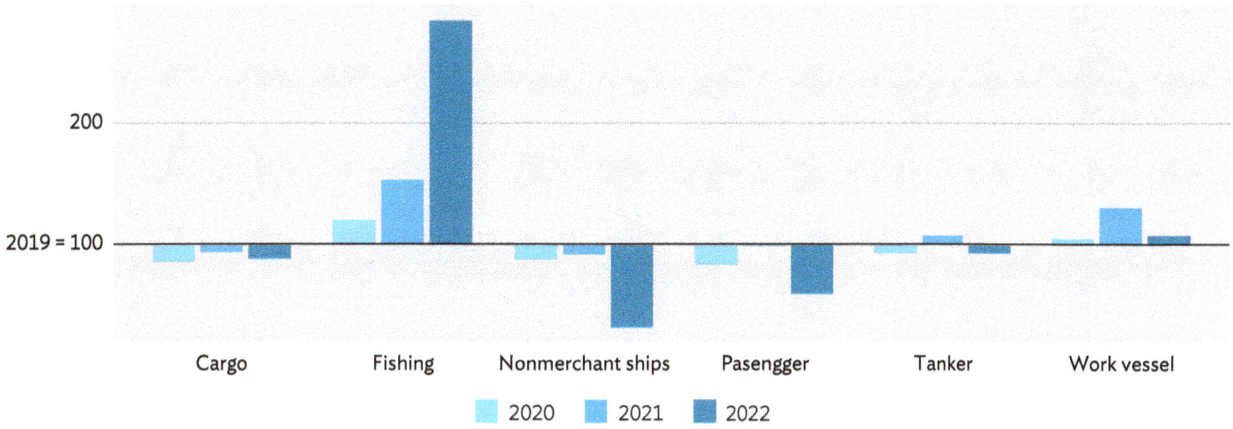

Note: Figures exclude category "Others" and "Unknown", which are arrivals from vessels without vessel type information from both UNGP-AIS and the Ship Registry dataset.
Source: Asian Development Bank calculations using United Nations Global Platform for Official Statistics. 2023. AIS Data. https://officialstatistics.org/ (accessed 31 August 2023).

Click here for figure data.

Complementing the port-level statistics are indicators on maritime highway transits whose construction is described in section 3.2. The relevant passageways for East Asia were determined to be the straits of Malacca and Singapore, which together connect East Asia with the western hemisphere. Each year, about 90,000 ships accounting for 40% of global trade cross these straits, making them a vital maritime artery not just for East Asia but for the world as a whole (Ough 2023). Figure 5.6 depicts vessel transits through these straits. Because of the changes in how AIS messages are recorded beginning 9 November 2021 (section 2.3), only data from that point on are plotted.

The Shanghai lockdowns did not appear to have much of an impact on vessel transits through these passageways, which speaks to the fact that they serve to connect more than just the Port of Shanghai. Other major ports in the region include Singapore, Busan in the Republic of Korea, and Kaohsiung in Taipei,China, not to mention Ningbo-Zhoushan, Shenzhen, Qingdao, and many more in the PRC itself. Data indicates that there has been a steady increase in traffic through these straits—in Malacca for example, daily traffic increased from an average of 230 in November 2021 to 250 by June 2023.

Figure 5.6: Daily Count of Unique Vessels, Straits of Malacca and Singapore, November 2021–June 2023

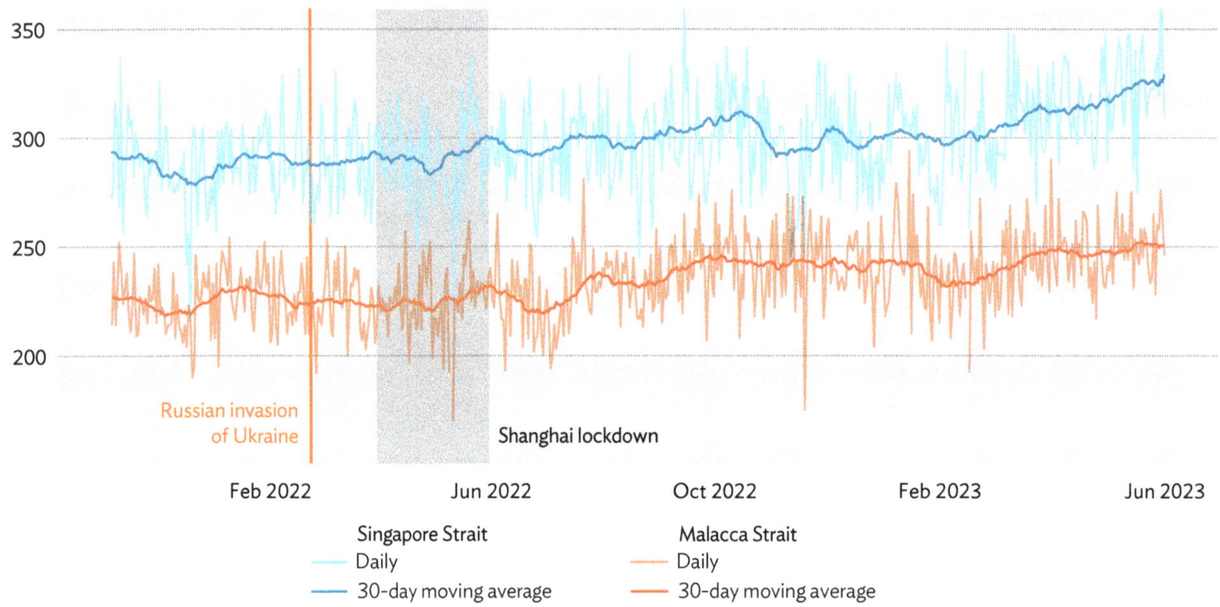

Notes:
1. Figure excludes dates affected by data quality issues (12 May 2022; 14 February 2023).
2. Shanghai lockdown: 1 April–1 June 2022.
3. Russian invasion of Ukraine: 24 February 2022.
Source: Asian Development Bank calculations using United Nations Global Platform for Official Statistics. 2023. AIS Data. https://officialstatistics.org/ (accessed 31 August 2023).

Click here for figure data.

5.2.2 Europe

The second region explored is Europe. The Port of Rotterdam is one of the most historic and prominent seaports of the continent. Holding the distinction of the world's busiest port from 1962 to 1986, Rotterdam's ranking was eventually surpassed by Asian ports like Singapore and Shanghai. Nevertheless, it maintains its strategic importance as a key distribution hub in the European continent due to its proximity to the German Ruhr district, Paris, London, and other densely populated and industrialized regions. It remains the largest seaport in Europe and assumes a pivotal role in facilitating trade across the continent (see Figure 5.7).

Figure 5.7: The Port of Rotterdam

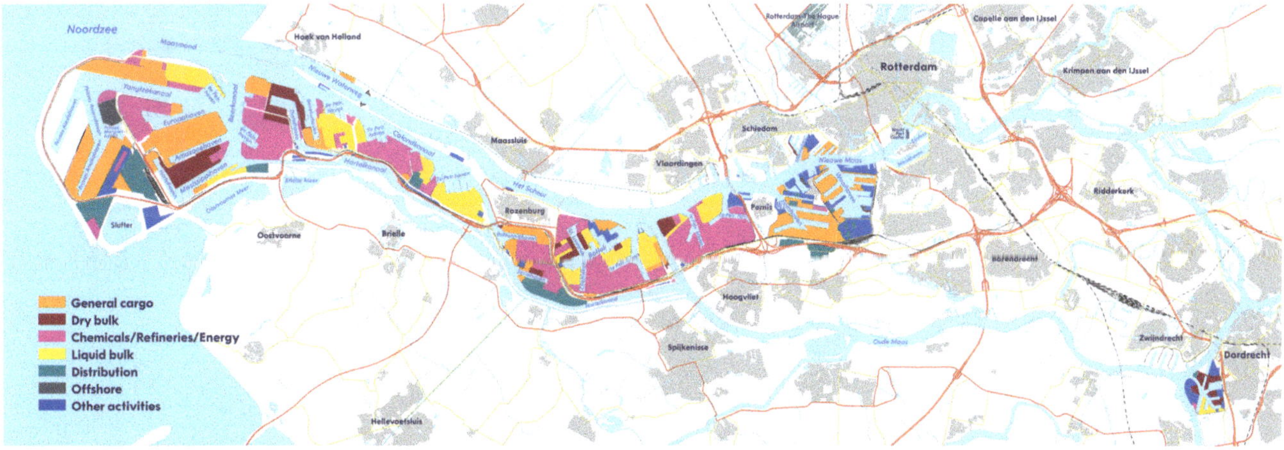

Note: The Port of Rotterdam is approximately 40 kilometers in length.
Source: Port of Rotterdam. 2022. Facts and Figures. https://www.portofrotterdam.com/en/experience-online/facts-and-figures (accessed 26 June 2023).

Click here for figure data.

The indicators derived for the Port of Rotterdam are depicted in the three panels of Figure 5.8. The daily counts of unique vessels within the port, shown in panel (a), appear to display much resilience in the face of global shocks, fluctuating around 1300 vessels throughout the period under study. The measure did take a dip following Italy's imposition of Europe's first pandemic-induced lockdown in March 2020, but in the context of its overall trend, this drop was not extraordinary. Neither was the Russian invasion of Ukraine enough to significantly disrupt vessel counts. As will be shown below, this stability is driven mainly by cargo and tanker vessels. The counts for passenger vessels, meanwhile, exhibited a greater impact.

Panels (b) and (c), respectively depicting daily vessel arrivals and median hours spent in the port, both also show only mild responses to the two shocks. Both indicators exhibited noticeable deviations right before the Italy lockdown, with daily arrivals dropping and median hours spiking. This preceded even the lockdowns in Hubei imposed by the PRC in January 2020.

Figure 5.8: Port Activity Indicators, Port of Rotterdam, 2019–2023

Notes:

1. Figures exclude dates affected by data quality issues (12 May 2022; 14 February 2023) and the start and end of the period (1 January 2019; 31 May 2023) for panels b and c.
2. Italy lockdown: 9 March–18 May 2020.
3. Russian invasion of Ukraine: 24 February 2022.

Source: Asian Development Bank calculations using United Nations Global Platform for Official Statistics. 2023. AIS Data. https://officialstatistics.org/ (accessed 31 August 2023).

Click here for figure data.

Table 5.2 shows that even with a longer time frame, the Port of Rotterdam showed resilience. All three indicators under consideration did not deviate drastically across the years. Where Rotterdam does finally exhibit some responses to shocks, however, is when looking at specific vessel categories. Figure 5.9 shows yearly arrivals for six categories of vessels, indexed to their levels in 2019. Cargo and tanker vessels, which comprise the bulk of total vessels, all showed minor deviations from 2019 levels. Fishing vessels, meanwhile, exhibited substantial drops. Fishing vessel arrivals to the Port of Rotterdam in 2021 were just half of what they were in 2019. Passenger and non-merchant ships have fared better, with arrivals rising from below to over 2019 levels by 2022. Work vessels were consistently above 2019 levels with little variation.

Table 5.2: Yearly Average of Daily Indicators, Port of Rotterdam, 2019–2022

	Count of Unique Vessels	Vessel Arrivals	Median Hours Spent
2019	1,279	370	24
2020	1,291	362	24
2021	1,334	371	25
2022	1,313	369	25

Source: Asian Development Bank calculations using United Nations Global Platform for Official Statistics. 2023. AIS Data. https://officialstatistics.org/ (accessed 31 August 2023).

Figure 5.9: Yearly Vessel Arrivals by Category, Port of Rotterdam, 2020–2022
(2019 = 100)

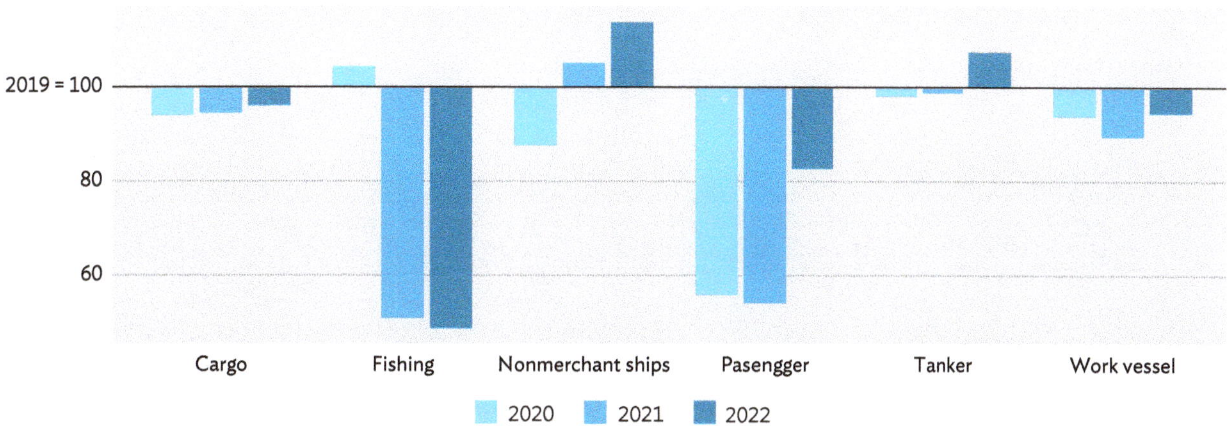

Note: Figure excludes vessel category 'Others' and 'Unknown' which are arrivals from vessels without vessel type information from both UNGP-AIS and Ship Registry dataset.
Source: Asian Development Bank calculations using United Nations Global Platform for Official Statistics. 2023. AIS Data and Ship Registry Dataset. https://officialstatistics.org/ (accessed 31 August 2023).

Click here for figure data.

The maritime highways associated with Europe in this report are the Strait of Gibraltar and the Suez Canal, which respectively connect the Mediterranean Sea to the Atlantic and Indian Oceans. In other words, they are the passageways that connect Europe's Mediterranean region to the Americas and Asia. While Gibraltar is a natural formation, the Suez Canal is artificial, a feat of engineering completed in 1869 that greatly reduced travel time by sea between Europe and Asia.

Much like the port-level indicators, Figure 5.10 shows that vessel transits through the Gibraltar and Suez passageways have proven resilient throughout the period under study. No deviation in vessel transit trends is apparent following Italy's lockdown in March 2020. While the blockage of the Suez Canal by the container ship *Ever Given* in March 2021 did halt traffic for six days, the impact was ultimately not enough to alter the measure's 30-day moving average. Transits in Gibraltar did rise following the Russian invasion of Ukraine in February 2022, caused potentially by the blockage of Ukraine's Black Sea ports, but this rise was not a large deviation from past trends.

Overall, maritime traffic in Europe—represented by the data related to the Port of Rotterdam, the Strait of Gibraltar, and the Suez Canal—has weathered the turbulent 2020–2022 period quite well. All indicators remained generally within historical trends. The largest deviations were those seen in daily arrivals to, and median time spent in,

Figure 5.10: Passageway Indicators, Strait of Gibraltar and Suez Canal, 2019–2023

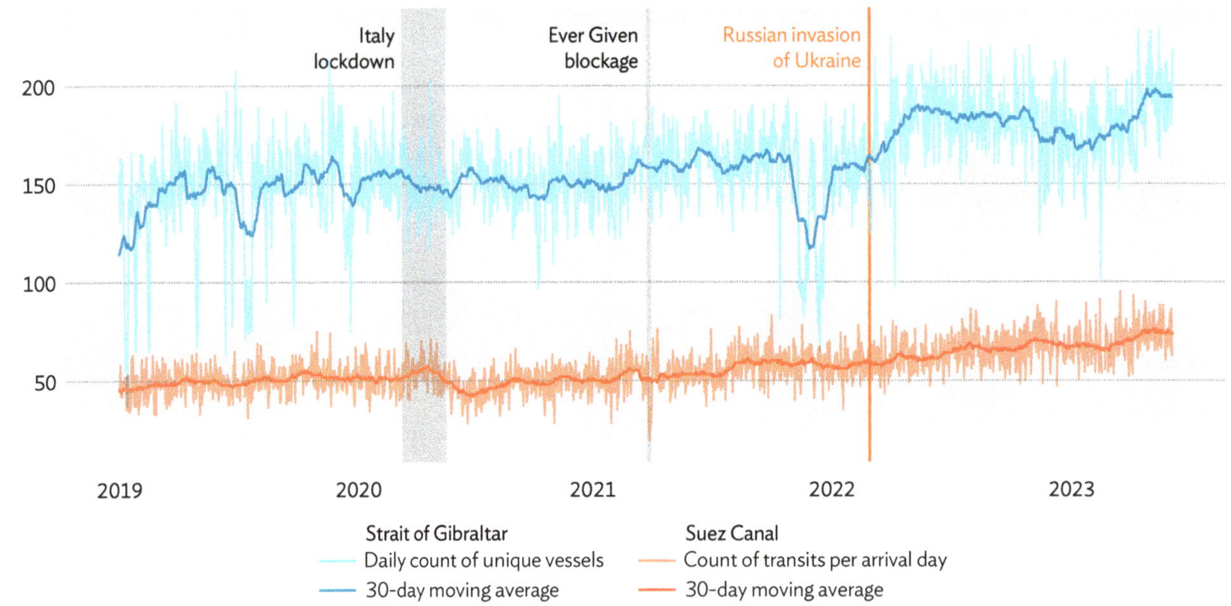

Notes:
1. Figure excludes dates affected by data quality issues (11–13 May 2022; 13–15 February 2023) and the start and end of the period (1 January 2019; 31 May 2023) for Suez Canal vessel transit.
2. Italy lockdown: 9 March–18 May 2020.
3. Ever Given blockage: 23–29 March 2021.
4. Russian invasion of Ukraine: 24 February 2022.

Source: Asian Development Bank calculations using United Nations Global Platform for Official Statistics. 2023. AIS Data. https://officialstatistics.org/ (accessed 31 August 2023).

Click here for figure data.

BOX 3

Impact of the Suez Canal Blockage on Maritime Activity

In 2021, the Suez Canal was blocked from 23 to 29 March by the Ever Given, one of the largest cargo ships in the world. The blockage stalled transits through the canal for nearly a week, causing delayed deliveries for vessels that opted to wait at the canal's entry and exit points, and for those that took a longer route around the Cape of Good Hope. While it is difficult to assess the total cost of the blockage on trade volume, indicators derived from AIS data can detect its impact on ship operations.

The figure below depicts how, from 1 January to 22 March, around 52 vessels per day on average would pass through the Suez Canal. By 26 March, the average transit count had plummeted to 22 vessels, dropping again the next day to 17 vessels. The next few days saw a rebound in transit count, mirroring actual events when some vessels deciding to re-route during this period. On the other hand, examining median transit time in the Suez Canal amplifies the impact of the blockage. For vessels that arrived on 22 March, the day before the blockage, median transit time jumped from 28 to 179 hours. The indicator gradually decreased until 7 April, more than a week after the Ever Given was dislodged.

Daily Transit Count and Median Transit Time for Suez Canal, Derived from AIS Data

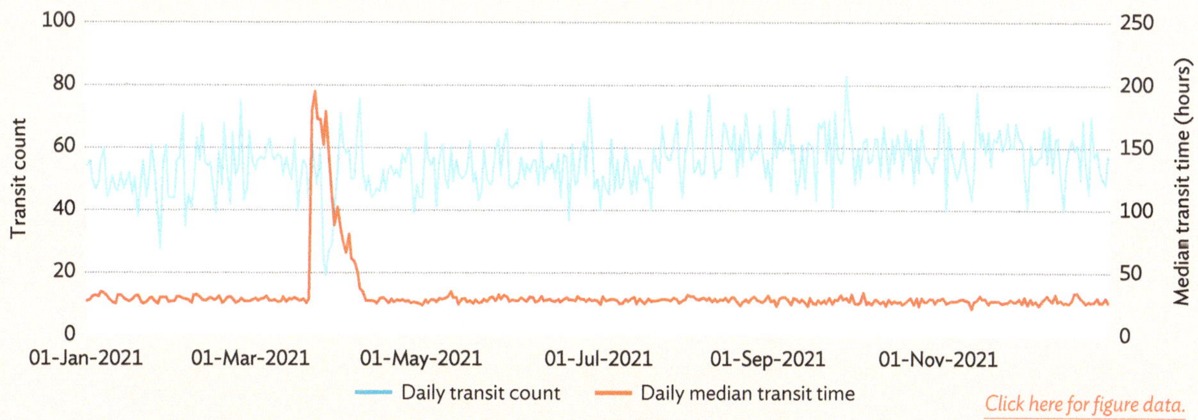

Click here for figure data.

Source: Asian Development Bank calculations using United Nations Global Platform for Official Statistics. 2023. AIS Data. https://officialstatistics.org/ (accessed 31 August 2023).

Rotterdam at the end of 2019, which do not yet have any identifiable causes and may perhaps be due to issues with the data. That aside, the maritime commerce of Europe can be said to be exceedingly resilient to external shocks.

5.2.3 The Americas

To represent the American continents, this report uses the twin ports of Los Angeles and Long Beach, here treated as a single entity (called LALB for short) due to their proximity even though they are managed by separate authorities (Figure 5.11). The two make up the largest in the western hemisphere, handling over 40% of all inbound containers for the entire United States (US). Their respective port authorities estimate the value of cargo handled in 2022 at $311 billion for Los Angeles and $200 billion for Long Beach, underscoring their importance as shipping and logistics hubs for international trade.

The three panels of Figure 5.12 show daily counts of unique vessel, daily arrivals, and

Figure 5.11: The Ports of Los Angeles and Long Beach

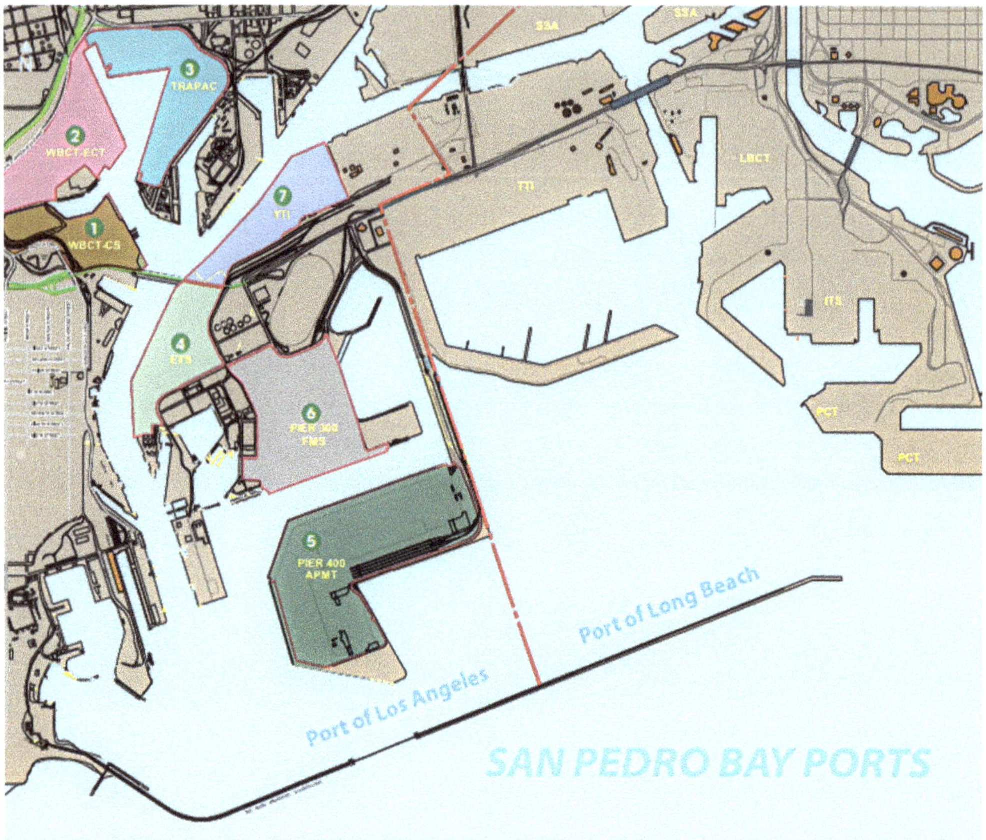

Note: The Ports of Los Angeles and Long Beach are directly adjacent to each other with just a wall serving as a boundary between them. However, despite their close proximity, they are managed by completely separate authorities.
Source: The Port of Los Angeles. https://kentico.portoflosangeles.org/getmedia/9d211240-85e0-4ea1-a52e-18b48fc6e1cc/2021-Four-Panel-Terminal-Map (accessed 26 June 2023)

Click here for figure data.

median time spent in the ports. Both unique counts and arrivals in panels (a) and (b) took dips during the initial COVID-19 lockdowns in Hubei. These, however, were not particularly significant relative to historical fluctuations. By late 2020, vessel counts began a sustained ascent, with 30-day averages peaking at just under 300 vessels a day in late 2021. Arrivals also began rising in this period, though to a lesser extent. This was a period of heightened port congestion, caused by consumers around the world shifting their spending from services to goods. In the US for example, goods as a share of household spending rose from 36% before the pandemic to 42% in spring 2021 (*The Economist* 2022). Imports arriving through the LALB ports, in particular, jumped 41.1% year-on-year in the first half of 2021; it handled 855,000 TEU per month on average between July 2020 and June 2021 against the 700,000 monthly average of 2019 (Mongeluzzo 2021).

Port congestion also manifests in median time spent in the ports, as depicted in panel (c). Two spikes occur in the series, the first in early 2020 and the second at the start of 2021. During these times, the median vessel spent over 30 hours in the LALB ports, compared with the 10–20 hours seen across the rest of the series. It appears however that port

Figure 5.12: Port Activity Indicators, Ports of Los Angeles and Long Beach, 2019–2023

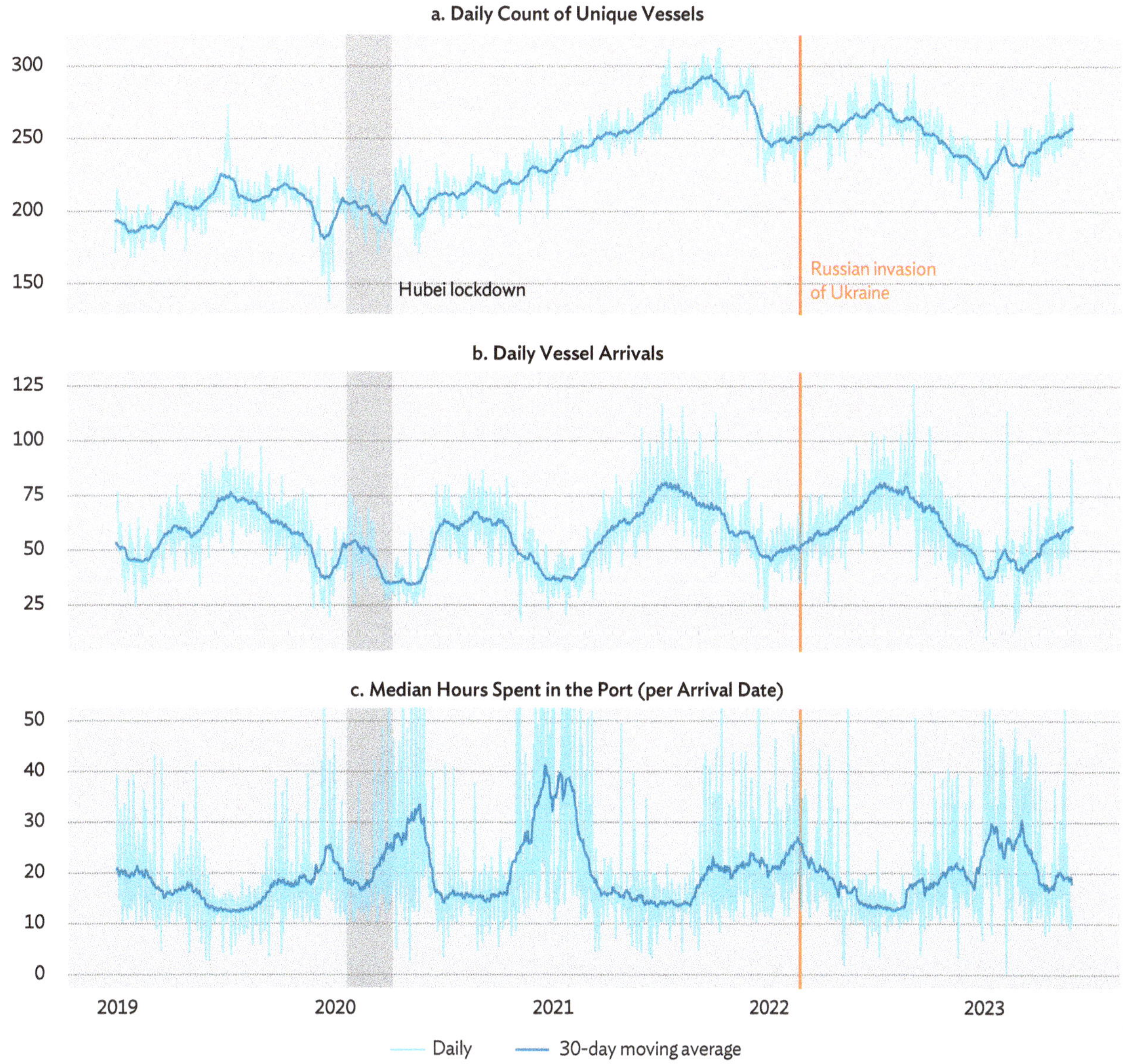

Notes:
1. Figures exclude dates affected by data quality issues (12 May 2022; 14 February 2023) and the start and end of the period (1 January 2019; 31 May 2023) for panels b and c.
2. Hubei lockdown: 23 January–8 April 2020.
3. Russian invasion of Ukraine: 24 February 2022.

Source: Asian Development Bank calculations using United Nations Global Platform for Official Statistics. 2023. AIS Data. https://officialstatistics.org/ (accessed 31 August 2023).

Click here for figure data.

congestion became less pressing by 2022, with median time returning to normal levels. Unique counts and arrivals also retreated in end-2022, though they remained elevated.

The yearly summary of the three indicators is presented in Table 5.3, where unique counts and arrivals are much higher in 2021–2022 compared to 2019–2020. Turning to yearly arrivals by vessel category, Figure 5.13 shows that cargo and tanker vessels remained close to where they were in 2019. The largest changes are seen in non-merchant ships, for which 2022 arrivals were 160% of 2019 levels, and passenger vessels, for which 2022 arrivals were just 84% of 2019 levels.

Table 5.3: Yearly Average of Daily Indicators, Ports of Los Angeles and Long Beach, 2019–2022

	Count of Unique Vessels	Vessel Arrivals	Median Hours Spent
2019	204	59	17
2020	212	51	22
2021	266	61	20
2022	255	63	18

Source: Asian Development Bank calculations using United Nations Global Platform for Official Statistics. 2023. AIS Data. https://officialstatistics.org/ (accessed 31 August 2023).

As the Americas are surrounded on either side by oceans, the single maritime passageway

Figure 5.13: Yearly Vessel Arrivals by Category, Ports of Los Angeles and Long Beach, 2020–2022 (2019 = 100)

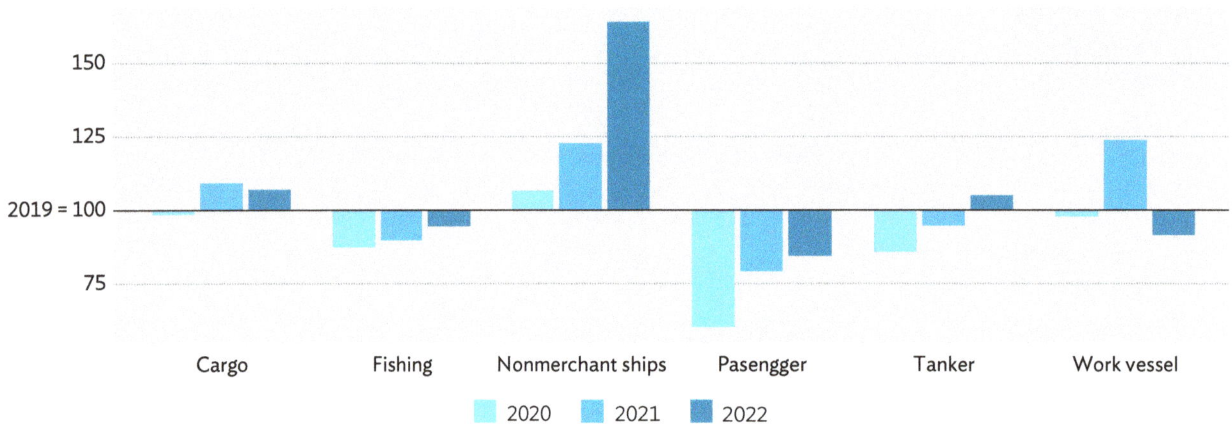

Note: Figure excludes vessel category 'Others' and 'Unknown' which are arrivals from vessels without vessel type information from both UNGP-AIS and Ship Registry dataset.
Source: Asian Development Bank calculations using United Nations Global Platform for Official Statistics. 2023. AIS Data and Ship Registry Dataset. https://officialstatistics.org/ (accessed 31 August 2023).

Click here for figure data.

associated with the two continents is the Panama Canal, through which ships cross from the Atlantic to the Pacific and vice versa. Opened in 1914, the Panama Canal cuts travel time significantly as ships would otherwise have to sail around the southernmost tip of South America.

The relatively stable trend depicted in Figure 5.14 demonstrates the resilience of maritime trade passing through the Panama Canal. There was a marked decrease at the onset of the COVID-19 lockdowns in early 2020, but transits quickly recovered and remained within a tight range throughout the years under study. This continued even after the Russian invasion of Ukraine in February 2022.

5.2.4 Middle East

BOX 4

Identifying Changes in Trend for Transit Indicator Using Changepoint Analysis

Changepoint analysis seeks to identify a point or points in a time-series during which a change, or break in the trend, takes place. This technique is applied to many social science questions where researchers need to understand the point in time a statistically significant change in the quantity being studied occurs. While time series of AIS indicators clearly indicate fluctuations, less obvious is the specific time at which a change occurred. Note that outliers are not necessarily changepoints, as changepoint analysis is concerned with changes in the overall trend rather than individual point-to-point variations.

This analysis aims to identify such points of change in AIS time series data. To achieve this, a changepoint model was built in R using the 'changepoint' package, which allows for multiple change points. The model requires an input of maximum number of changepoints to search for which is critical in the analysis. A key consideration is the trade-off between model complexity (number of changepoints) and model fit. A more complex model with more changepoints may fit the data better, but it could also lead to overfitting. Therefore, explanatory data analysis is carried out first to get a deeper understanding of the data patterns. Statistics on trade activities from other major ports are also referred to so as to inform the study. After careful consideration of these factors, the maximum number of changepoints to search for is set as four in the model. The model was then applied to the daily count of unique vessels, daily arrivals, and median time spent for the ports of Los Angeles and Long Beach (LALB). The detected changepoints are shown in the figure below.

Figure a shows the count of unique vessels with three changepoints, dividing the time series data into four periods. The first period spans 2019 to 2020. Notably, no change was detected during the start of COVID-19. By 2021, two change points emerged at the start and middle of the year, marking a higher average daily count of unique vessels which coincides with reported congestion in the ports. By 2022, though, the average had returned to the same level as in the first half of 2021, suggesting an overall increase in port activities.

The effect of the COVID-19 pandemic seems to be captured in vessel arrivals (Figure b), as changepoints are detected by late 2019 and early 2021. The average count of daily arrivals from 2019 decreased by 2020 and returned to baseline by 2021. There is another changepoint by the end of 2022 resulting in a lower average count like that seen in 2020. In Figure c concerning the median time spent in the port, only the spike seen in late 2020 caused a changepoint. This suggests that the spikes in median time during early 2020 are not as significant as the spike seen later in the year.

Thus, it is a reasonable deduction that the ports of LALB witnessed significant congestion from the end of 2020 to early 2021.

Identified Change Points for the Ports of Los Angeles and Long Beach

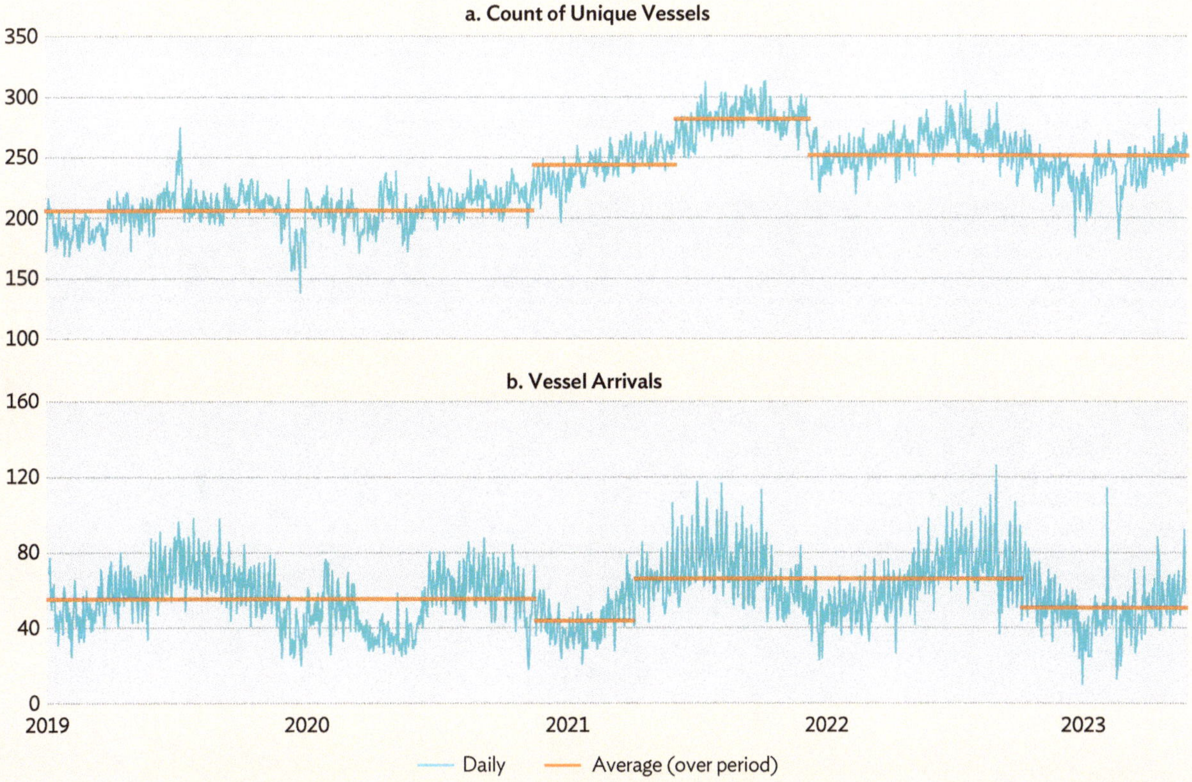

continued on next page.

Box 4 *continued.*

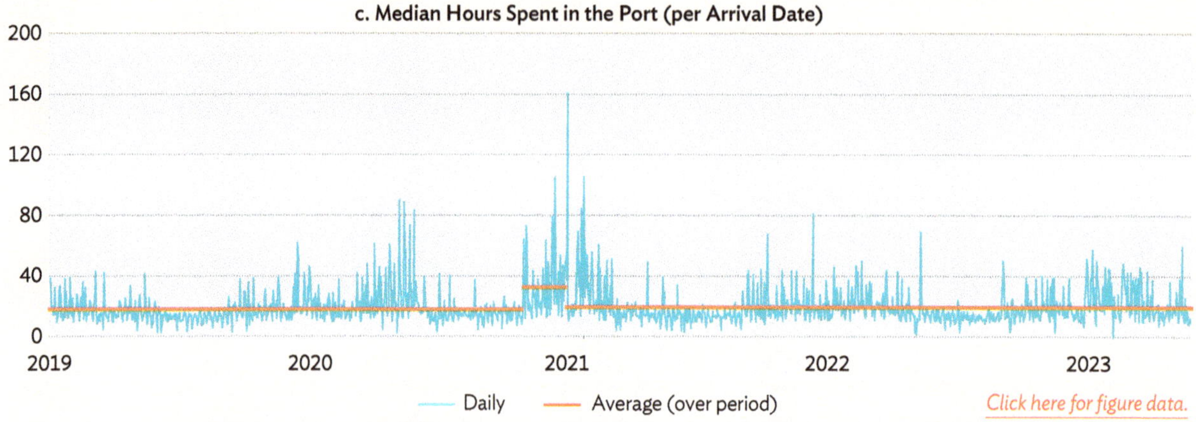

Click here for figure data.

Source: Asian Development Bank calculations using United Nations Global Platform for Official Statistics. 2023. AIS Data. https://officialstatistics.org/ (accessed 31 August 2023).
Reference: R. Killick, I. A. Eckley. 2014. changepoint: An R Package for Changepoint Analysis. Journal of Statistical Software, 58(3), 1–19. https://www.jstatsoft.org/article/view/v058i03.

Figure 5.14: Daily Vessel Transits, Panama Canal, 2019–2023

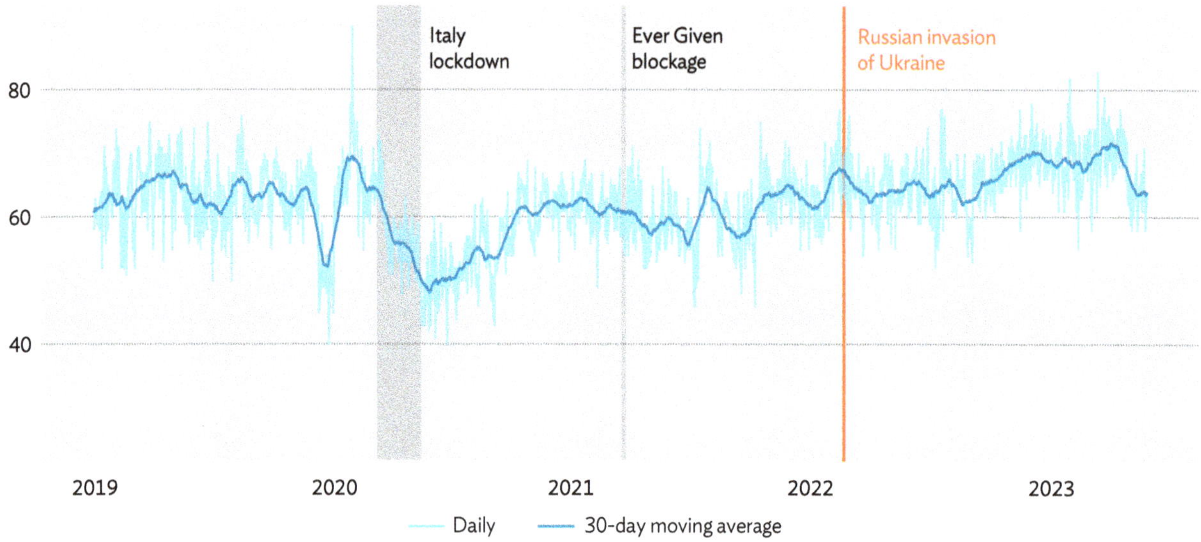

Notes:
1. Figure excludes dates affected by data quality issues (12 May 2022; 14 February 2023).
2. Italy lockdown period: 9 March–18 May 2020.
3. Ever Given blockage: 23–29 March 2021.
4. Russian invasion of Ukraine: 24 February 2022.

Source: Asian Development Bank calculations using United Nations Global Platform for Official Statistics. 2023. AIS Data. https://officialstatistics.org/ (accessed 31 August 2023).

Click here for figure data.

The Russian invasion of Ukraine in February 2022 upended the global market for commodities, particularly those of oil and gas. For this reason, it is worthwhile to briefly examine what impact the invasion might have had on maritime traffic around the Middle East, a region that accounts for 31.3% of global oil production (bp 2022). Transit statistics were therefore computed for the straits of Hormuz and Bab el-Mandeb, which respectively serve as the entrances to the Persian Gulf and the Red Sea. Through these straits pass the oil tankers of Saudi Arabia, Iraq, and the United Arab Emirates, among others.

Figure 5.15 shows that traffic along these maritime corridors increased after the invasion, though not to any dramatic extent. Transits through the Strait of Hormuz are strongly seasonal, falling toward the end of the year before rising again in the middle of the year. After the invasion, 30-day averages for transits exceeded 100 vessels a day, something that did not occur in 2019–2021. Nevertheless, it did not alter the seasonal trend of the series. The Bab el-Mandeb Strait, on the other hand, has traffic that is more stable. Transits here picked up slightly after the invasion, though admittedly they had been on an upward trend since 2021. Overall, despite the heightened volatility in oil prices in the months after the invasion, AIS-derived maritime statistics paint a relatively subdued picture.

Figure 5.15: Daily Vessel Transits, Straits of Hormuz and Bab el-Mandeb, 2019–2023

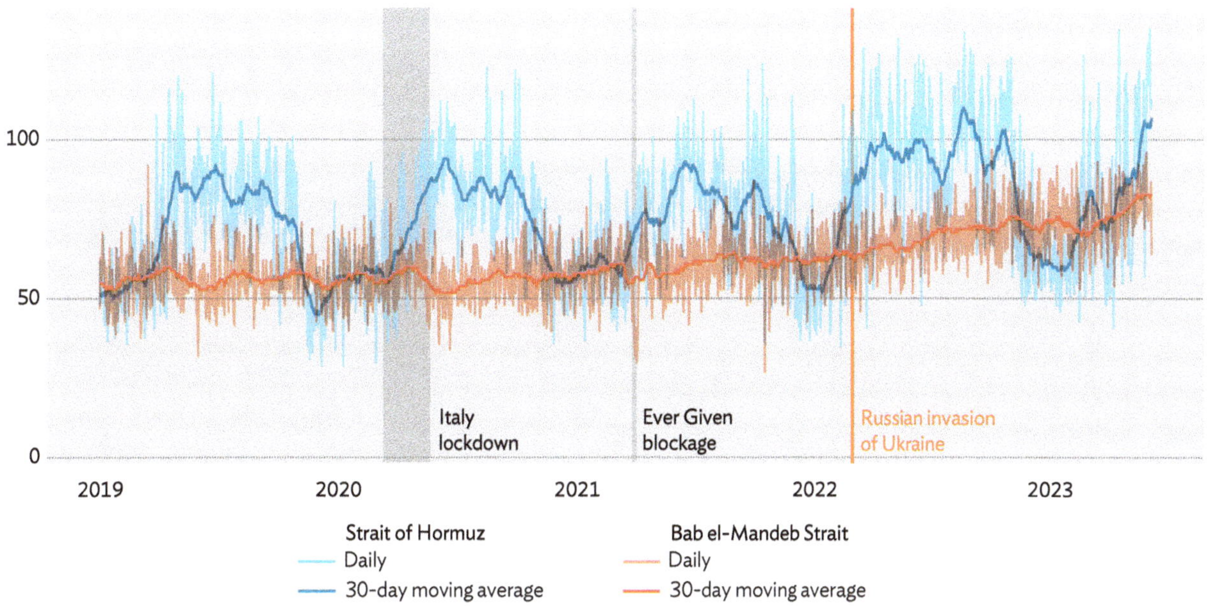

Note:
1. Figure excludes dates affected by data quality issues (12 May 2022; 14 February 2023).
2. Italy lockdown period: 9 March–18 May 2020.
3. Ever Given blockage: 23–29 March 2021.
4. Russian invasion of Ukraine: 24 February 2022.
Source: Asian Development Bank calculations using United Nations Global Platform for Official Statistics. 2023. AIS Data. https://officialstatistics.org/ (accessed 31 August 2023).

Click here for figure data.

5.3 Validation

The final section of this chapter undertakes a validation exercise for some of the indicators in this report by comparing them against alternative data sources, either AIS-derived or official statistics from port or canal authorities. While there may be notable discrepancies between the statistics provided in this publication and relevant AIS-derived indicators compiled by other data providers, likely due to methodological differences, the estimates appear to be highly coherent with official data, displaying absolute percentage errors of just 3%-4%. These are highly encouraging results that validate the use of AIS data to generate timely, accurate and relevant maritime statistics.

Figure 5.16: Comparison of Arrivals with Alternative Automatic Identification System-Based Indicators, Ports of Shanghai and Rotterdam

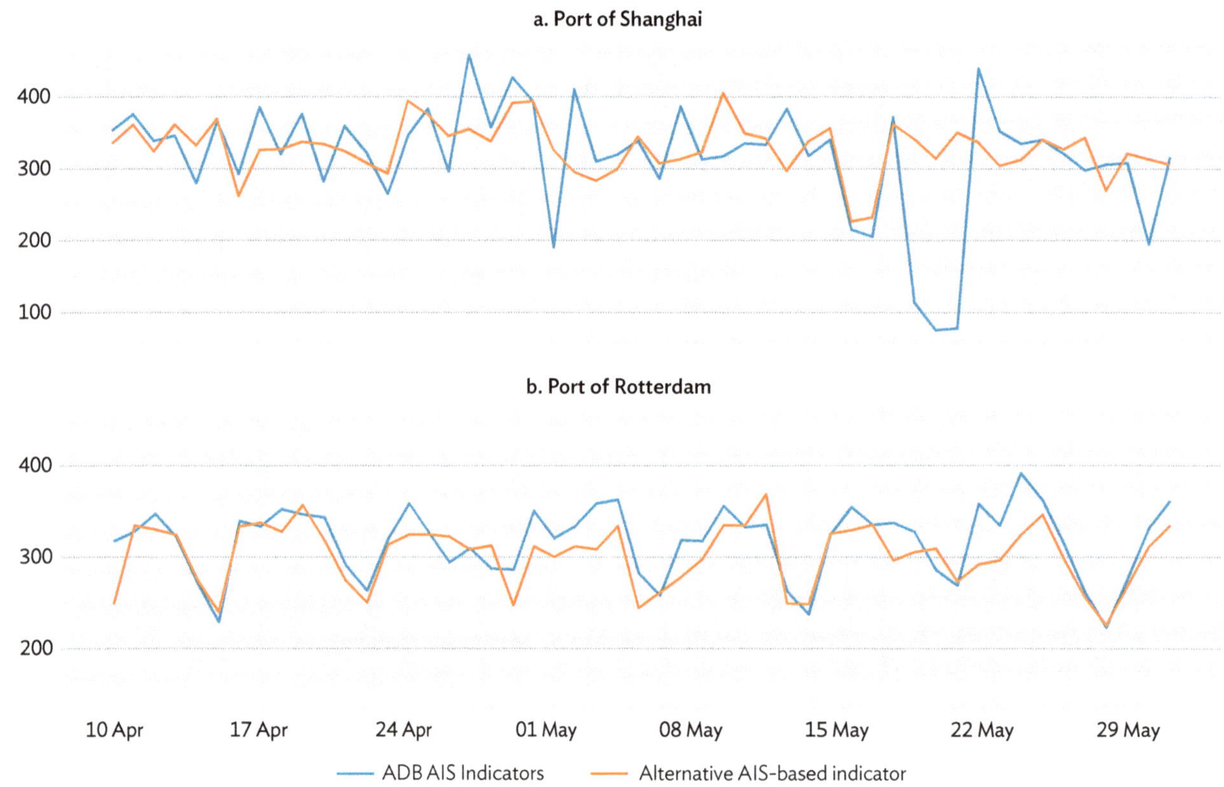

ADB = Asian Development Bank, AIS = Automatic Identification System.
Sources: Asian Development Bank calculations using United Nations Global Platform for Official Statistics. 2023. AIS Data. https://officialstatistics.org/ (accessed 31 August 2023); Marine Traffic. 2023. Rotterdam Port Arrivals Data. https://www.marinetraffic.com/en/ais/details/ports/2036?name=ROTTERDAM&country=Netherlands (accessed 21 June 2023); and MyShipTracking. 2023. Shanghai Port Arrivals Data. https://www.myshiptracking.com/ports/port-of-shanghai-in-cn-china-id-4119 (accessed 21 June 2023).

Click here for figure data.

Other data providers have used the AIS to track the same indicators as this report. It is therefore of interest to see how they compare. Figure 5.16 plots daily vessel arrivals to the ports of Shanghai and Rotterdam as measured by this report and by private data providers MyShipTracking (for Shanghai) and MarineTraffic (for Rotterdam). It covers 51 days over April–May 2023. For Shanghai, the mean absolute percentage error (MAPE) is quite large at 28.1%, though much of the error comes from three days in May 2023 when this report's measure recorded a significant drop in arrivals whereas MyShipTracking did not. Excluding these days, the MAPE falls to 11.7%. For Rotterdam on the other hand, the MAPE is much smaller at 6.4%. The notable discrepancies seen here are likely due to differences in methodologies given that the same fundamental data is being used. As mentioned in section 3.1.1, defining port boundaries is nontrivial as different approaches can potentially lead to very different results. In particular, note that the discrepancies for Shanghai, where port boundaries are less well defined due to their noncontiguous nature, are larger than those for Rotterdam which has a more compact port.

Further, Figure 5.17 uses officially published statistics to compare arrivals with the measures in this report. Comparisons are made for the ports of LALB, the Suez Canal, and the Panama Canal. Because these are official statistics, they are only available at lower frequencies—yearly for the LALB ports and monthly for the two canals. Moreover, Suez Canal statistics are only available up to January 2020 while Panama Canal statistics are missing March and April 2020. It is in such scenarios where AIS-derived indicators can be especially useful given their higher frequencies and greater completeness.

Of the four years under consideration for the LALB ports, this report's vessel arrivals measure recorded a MAPE of 4.0% against official data. The largest discrepancy was in 2019; moreover, the AIS-derived indicator tends to overestimate annual arrivals. Nevertheless, the error is overall relatively small. Measures for transits through the Suez and Panama canals were likewise respectable, recording MAPEs of 3.2% and 3.1%, respectively, against official data. All these are highly promising results that suggest that AIS-derived indicators can indeed complement officially published statistics without significant loss of accuracy.

The analyses undertaken in this chapter demonstrate that the indicators generated accurately reflect significant events affecting the specific ports, including congestion in the LALB ports throughout 2021, and COVID-19 lockdown measures implemented in Shanghai from March to May 2022. Results reveal that AIS-derived indicators are consistent with relevant official data, underscoring the potential of AIS as an alternative data source for maritime statistics. AIS-derived transit statistics from the Suez Canal and the Panama Canal were almost identical to official figures, while AIS-derived port statistics for LALB ports follow the trend from official data.

The potential of AIS data as an alternative source of maritime statistics lies in its high

Figure 5.17: Comparison of Arrivals with Official Statistics, Ports of Los Angeles and Long Beach, Suez Canal, and Panama Canal

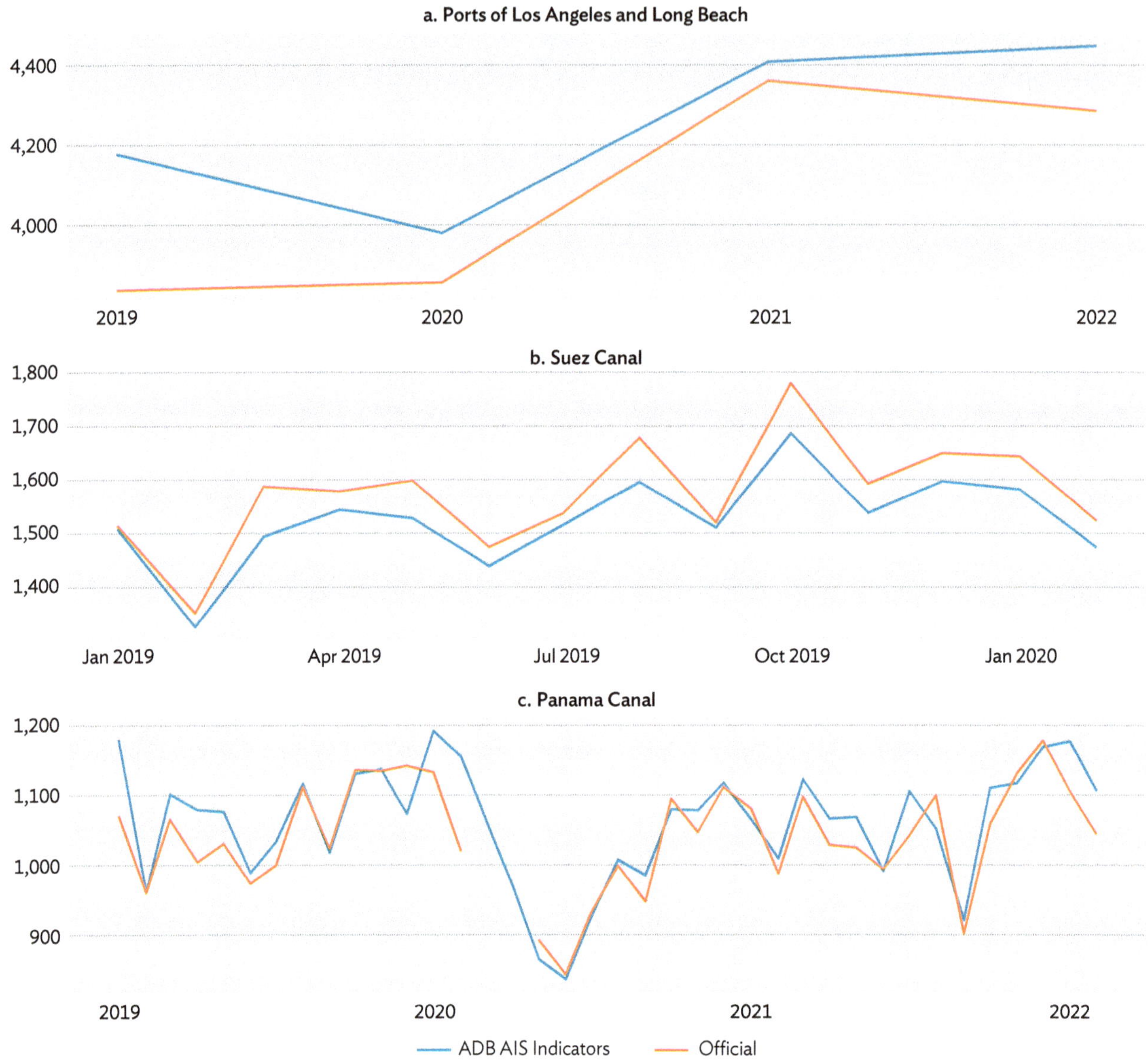

ADB = Asian Development Bank, AIS = Automatic Identification System.

Note: Figures for March and April 2020 from Panama Canal Authority are not available.

Sources: Asian Development Bank calculations using United Nations Global Platform for Official Statistics. 2023. AIS Data. https://officialstatistics.org/ (accessed 31 August 2023); Panama Canal Authority. 2022. Transit Statistics. https://pancanal.com/en/statistics/; The Port of Los Angeles. 2022. *Facts and Figures*. https://www.portoflosangeles.org/business/statistics/facts-and-figures (accessed 26 June 2023); The Port of Long Beach. 2022. *Annual Comprehensive Financial Report*. https://polb.com/business/finance/#annual-reports-acfr (accessed 26 June 2023); and Suez Canal Authority. 2020. Navigation reports. https://www.suezcanal.gov.eg/English/Downloads/Pages/default.aspx?folder=Navigation+Reports.

Click here for figure data.

Chapter 6

Understanding Maritime Activity Disruptions Using Automatic Identification System Data

frequency and near real-time availability, allowing for varying levels of time aggregation depending on the target analysis. This chapter presents daily aggregations of the AIS indicators for maritime hubs discussed in Chapter 5. This alternate view of the indicators serves to highlight the impact of recent disruptions to major ports caused by war (Port of Odesa in Ukraine), economic crisis (Port of Colombo in Sri Lanka), and disaster (Port of Nuku'alofa in Tonga).

The analysis aims to determine if AIS data can be used to generate high-frequency and timely indicators for disruptions to maritime and trade activity. The indicators generated cover various aspects of port activity, such as the count of ships within specific Areas of Interest (AOIs), the number of ship arrivals, and the duration of time spent in port. In addition, the count of unique vessels indicator was further investigated according to three ship categories: trade-related vessels (encompassing cargo and tanker categories, see Table 3.1), passenger-related vessels (consisting of roll-on/roll-off or RORO passenger, passenger, and cruise ships), and naval ships. Due to the absence of predefined areas for the three ports under consideration, the cluster-based approach discussed in section 3.1.1 was used to establish these areas of interest. The indicators are available in the database accompanying this publication.

6.1 Disruptions Due to War

With an annual capacity of about 40 million tons, the Port of Odesa is the largest seaport in Ukraine and one of the largest in the Black Sea region. The port houses oil, grain, transit-cargo, and passenger terminals. The Russian invasion of Ukraine in February 2022 severely disrupted maritime activity in the Black Sea. A naval blockade halted the operation of vessels at the Port of Odesa, leading to hundreds of vessels being trapped in ports or at anchor (Allianz Global Corporate & Specialty 2022).

To examine if AIS data can capture this downturn in port activity, two passageways leading to the Black Sea were investigated: the Dardanelles Strait and the Bosphorus Strait. Vessels traveling from the Mediterranean Sea to the Black Sea would have to traverse the Dardanelles Strait, then the Bosphorus strait. Figure 6.1a shows the daily count of unique vessels passing through the Dardanelles strait, which even before the Russian invasion of Ukraine had been trending downward from October 2021 to February 2022. In the Bosphorus strait, meanwhile, the number of vessels dropped right after the Russian invasion of Ukraine, but promptly recovered over the next few months (Figure 6.1b). Figure 6.1c likewise depicts the sharp decrease in the count of unique ships heralded by the invasion, albeit with a recovery by the third quarter of 2022.

Figure 6.1: Daily Count of Unique Vessels, Dardanelles Strait, Bosphorus Strait, and Port of Odesa, 2019–2023

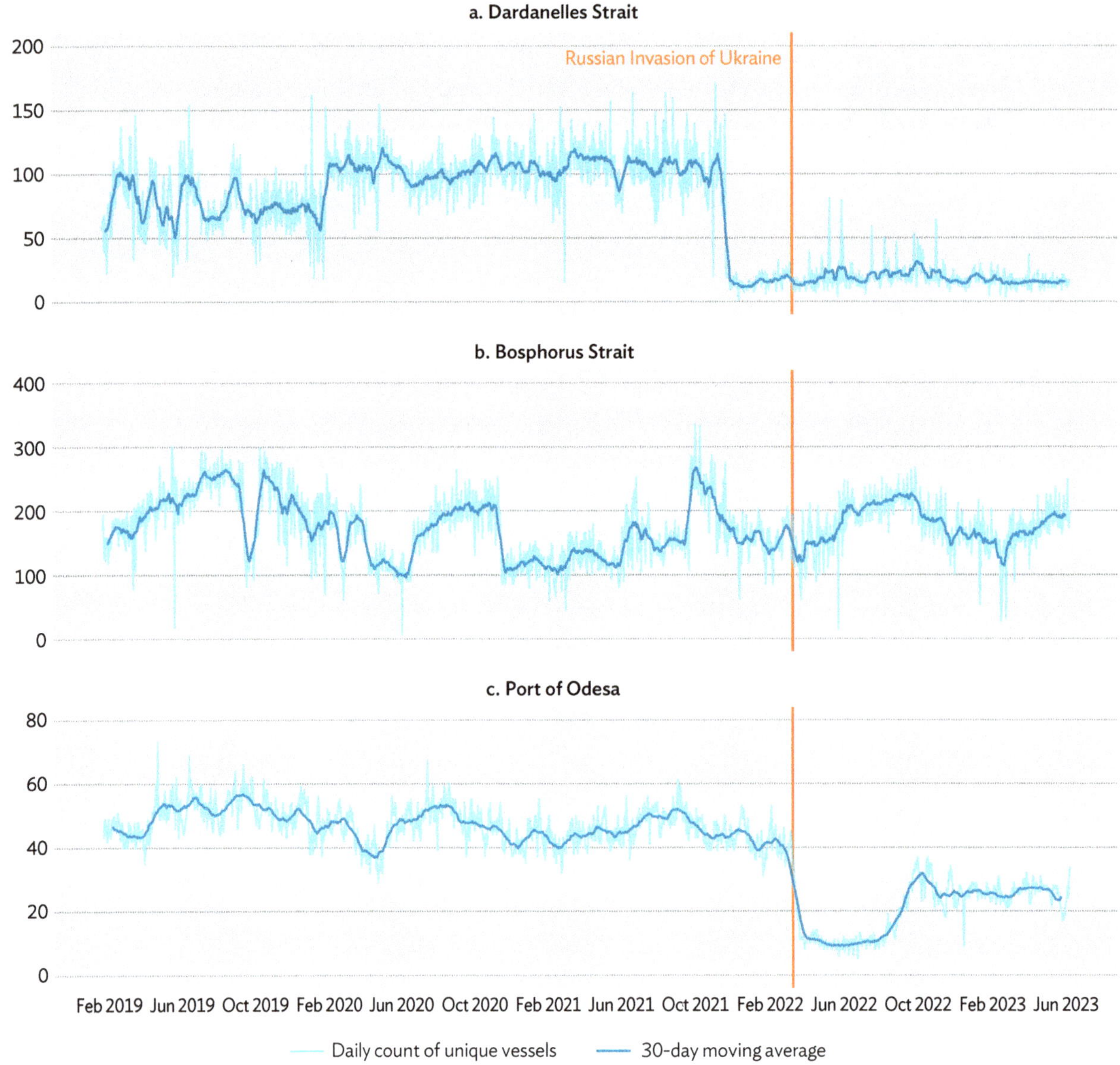

Notes:
1. Figure excludes dates affected by data quality issues (12 May 2022; 14 February 2023).
2. Russian invasion of Ukraine; 24 February 2022.
Source: Asian Development Bank calculations using United Nations Global Platform for Official Statistics. 2023. AIS Data. https://officialstatistics.org/ (accessed 31 August 2023).

Click here for figure data.

Figure 6.2a depicts the daily count of unique trade-related vessels. The Port of Odesa witnessed a sharp drop in the number of trade-related ships in March 2022, reflecting the adverse impact of the invasion on maritime operations. However, a recovery was apparent by July 2022, signaled by a gradual improvement in trade-related ship activity. This uptrend may be associated with the signing of the Black Sea Grain Initiative in July 2022, an agreement among Ukraine, the Russian Federation, Türkiye, and the United Nations which facilitated the reopening of Black Sea shipping routes.

Figure 6.2b shows the daily count of passenger-related vessels. The figure reveals fluctuations in the number of passenger-related vessels in the Port of Odesa from 2019 to 2021 before plummeting in February 2022. A more detailed investigation showed that no cruise ships have docked in the port since April 2022, and no RORO passenger vessels have been detected. This strongly indicates the injurious impact of the Russian invasion of Ukraine on passenger-related maritime traffic in the port. Taken together, these figures demonstrate how AIS data can be translated into indicators that capture and help decision makers understand disruptions in maritime traffic, international trade, and even tourism—in the case of passenger-related vessels.

Figure 6.2: Daily Count of Unique Vessels by Category, Port of Odesa, 2019–2023

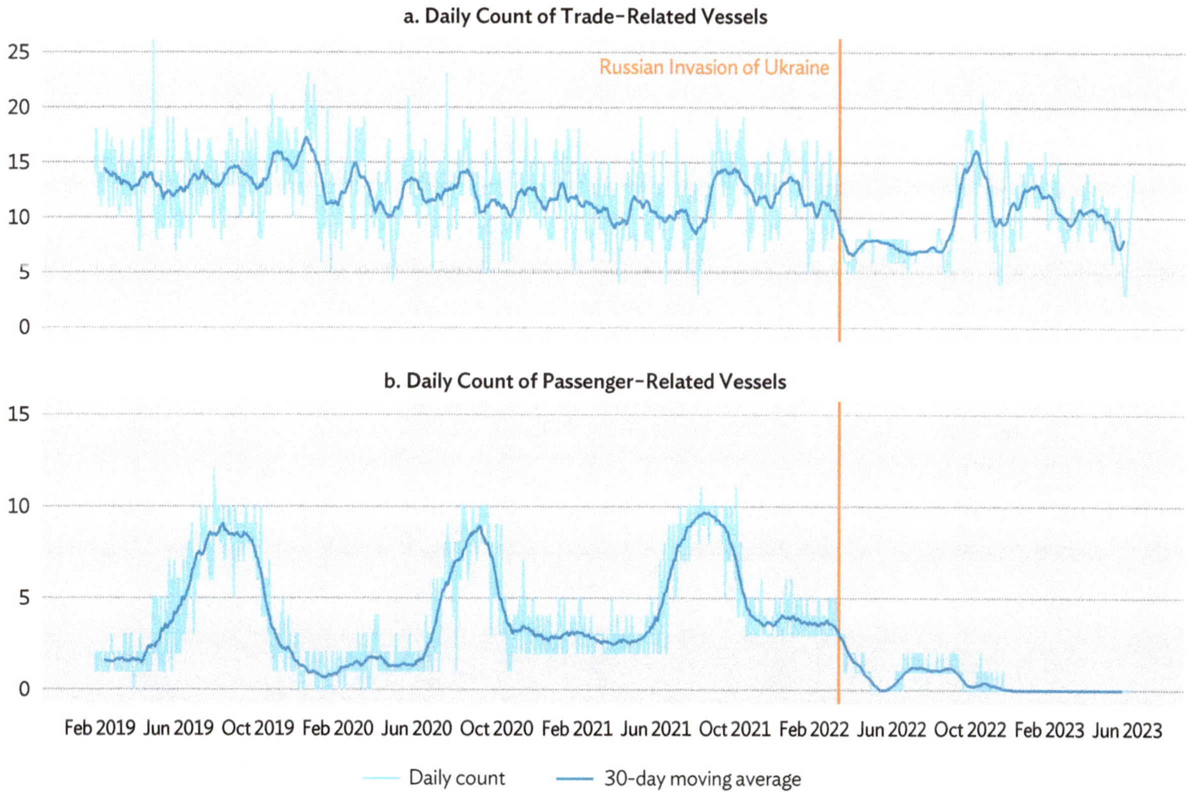

Notes:

1. Figure excludes dates affected by data quality issues (12 May 2022; 14 February 2023). Trade-related vessels consist of cargo and tanker categories (see Table 3.1).
2. Russian invasion of Ukraine: 24 February 2022.

Source: Asian Development Bank calculations using United Nations Global Platform for Official Statistics. 2023. AIS Data and Ship Registry Dataset. https://officialstatistics.org/ (accessed 31 August 2023).

Click here for figure data.

6.2 Disruptions Due to Economic Crisis

Sri Lanka has faced severe challenges with its balance of payments and debt since early 2022 (Asian Development Bank 2023). Foreign exchange reserves dropped significantly, causing a sharp rise in inflation and a drastic depreciation of the local currency. Critical shortages of essential goods like food, medicine, and fuel catalyzed an economic and humanitarian crisis, jeopardizing the country's poverty reduction gains since the end of the civil war in 2009. The Sri Lankan economy contracted by 7.8% in 2022, prompting political leadership changes due to widespread unrest.

The Port of Colombo is Sri Lanka's key transshipment hub and the largest port in Sri Lanka. A rapidly growing container port and maritime hub in South Asia, its monthly port calls reach 370 vessels on average. Among South Asian ports in 2021, Port of Colombo registered the highest Liner Shipping Connectivity Index (LSCI), which measures how well economies are connected to global shipping networks based on the status of their maritime transport sector (United Nations Conference on Trade and Development 2022).[9] Port operations have been largely unaffected by the economic crisis (Meade 2022), with port calls remaining steady since 2019—yet export and import volumes have declined by 1.8% and 11.9% respectively since the start of 2022. The succeeding paragraphs investigate if AIS-derived indicators reflect such changes in vessel volume not otherwise captured by port calls.

Despite the ongoing economic crisis in Sri Lanka, there is no substantial change in the count of unique vessels from 2019 to 2022 (Figure 6.3). When visualized by vessel category, Figure 6.4a likewise shows a stable trend for the daily count of trade-related vessels. Passenger-related vessel counts, meanwhile, fluctuated over time (Figure 6.4b). Investigation of trends at a more granular vessel level showed a relatively high number of cruise ships in 2019 before dropping in 2020, with a sustained downtrend until 2022. Further, no RORO passenger vessels appeared in the port in 2020.

9 The higher a country's index, the greater access to overseas markets a country has. UNCTAD reports quarterly values of the LSCI.

Figure 6.3: Daily Count of Unique Vessels, Port of Colombo, 2019–2023

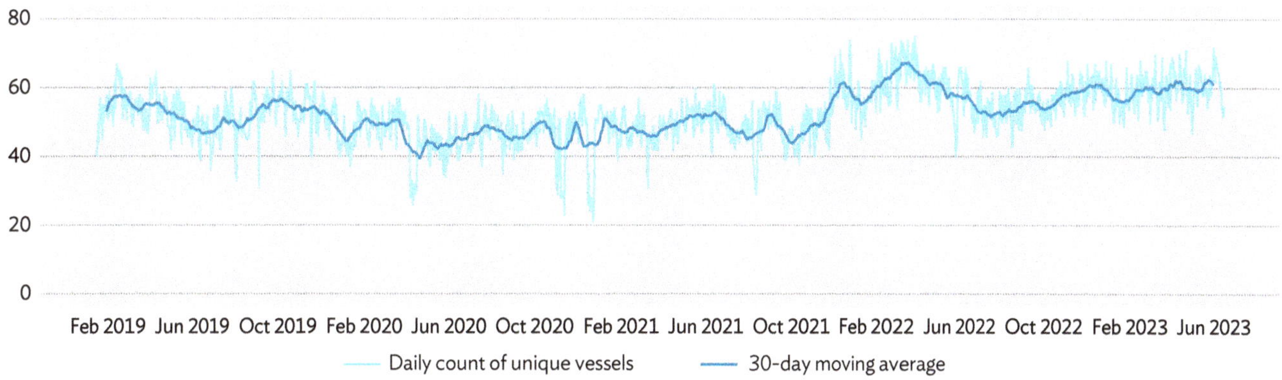

Note: Figure excludes dates affected by data quality issues (12 May 2022; 14 February 2023).
Source: Asian Development Bank calculations using United Nations Global Platform for Official Statistics. 2023. AIS Data. https://officialstatistics.org/ (accessed 31 August 2023).

Click here for figure data.

Figure 6.4: Daily Count of Unique Vessels by Category, Port of Colombo, 2019–2023

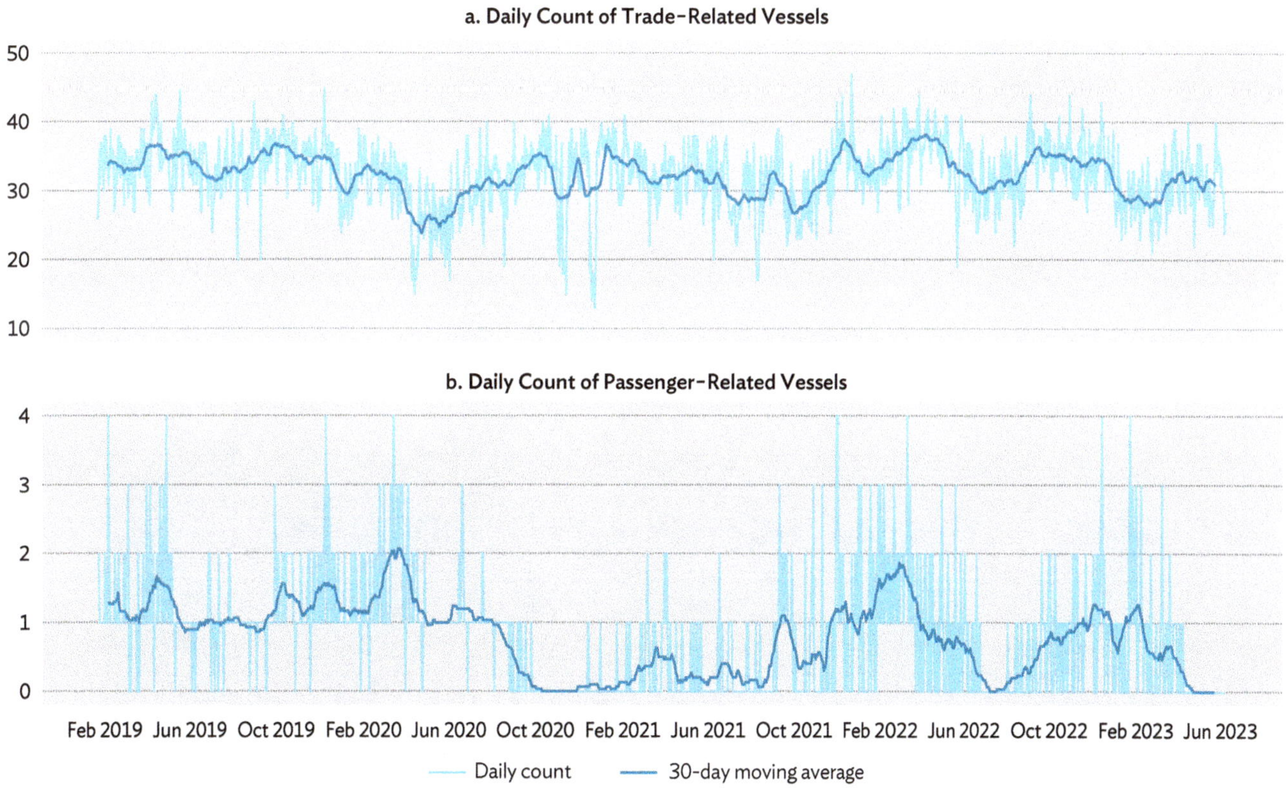

Notes: Figure excludes dates affected by data quality issues (12 May 2022; 14 February 2023). Trade-related vessels consist of cargo and tanker categories (see Table 3.1).
Source: Asian Development Bank calculations using United Nations Global Platform for Official Statistics. 2023. AIS Data and Ship Registry Dataset. https://officialstatistics.org/ (accessed 31 August 2023).

Click here for figure data.

6.3 Disruptions Due to Disasters

The Kingdom of Tonga, commonly known as Tonga, is an archipelagic country in the South Pacific Ocean. In January 2022, Tonga's Hunga Tonga-Hunga Ha'apai volcano erupted, becoming one of the biggest in recorded history. The volcanic eruption triggered tsunamis reaching 65 feet above sea level, sweeping Tongan islands and destroying hundreds of structures in its wake (Pacific Coastal and Marine Center 2022). A satellite image of the eruption can be seen in Figure 6.5.

Planes and ships from Australia and New Zealand flocked immediately to the Port of Nuku'alofa, Tonga's main port, to provide relief and aid operations (Menon and Needham 2022). The eruption wrought an estimated $20.9 million in damage to infrastructure, including ports and marine and water supply infrastructure (World Bank 2022). Maritime activity in the Nuku'alofa port was severely disrupted. The succeeding section explores if AIS data can produce indicators that capture the impact of the eruption on maritime activity. The analysis attempts to observe (i) an increase in the number and variation in vessel types in the port, owing to the arrival of rescue and relief ships; and (ii) a decrease in relief-related maritime activity, a possible indication of recovery. If AIS can accurately reflect changes in maritime activity due to disasters, then an argument can be made of its ability to provide timelier alternative indicators of maritime activity compared to official statistics, which typically follow an annual release schedule.

Figure 6.5: Satellite Image of the Eruption of Hunga Tonga-Hunga Ha'apai Volcano on 15 January 2022

Source: NASA Earth Observatory image by Joshua Stevens using GOES imagery courtesy of NOAA and NESDIS. https://www.nasa.gov/sites/default/files/thumbnails/image/tonga_goes_2022015_4k.gif.

Click here for figure data.

Evolution of AIS density on the Port of Nuku'alofa

The Port of Nuku'alofa serves as the central hub for transport, international import, and export cargo shipping in Tonga, supporting container, RORO vessels, general cargo, and tanker ships. Its four international wharfs receive around 200 port calls per year. A heatmap of how AIS messages evolved in the Port of Nuku'alofa from December 2021 to April 2022 reveals changes in density during the volcanic eruption (Figure 6.6).

The heatmap for December 2021 portrays the business-as-usual scenario for the port given a ship distribution during regular operations (Figure 6.6a). Significant changes then occur in January 2022 marked by an increased number of ships appearing in the berth and anchorage areas beyond 5 km radius (Figure 6.6b). By February 2022, the volcanic eruption heralds an influx of ship activity, which might be attributed to the arrival of rescue and naval ships (Figure 6.6c). Activity gradually tapers off by March 2022 (Figure 6.6d), and by April 2022 the ship distribution had returned to the business-as-usual concentration.

The changes in port activity during the volcanic eruption reveal that a fixed boundary, whether at 2km or 5km, is insufficient to make sense of an evolving situation. This highlights the advantages of using a cluster-based AOI to identify new areas of activity in similar cases. Further, even for ports with stable activities, cluster-based AOIs would still provide reasonably accurate of the minimum radius needed to cover all port activities.

Analyzing trends in the number of unique vessels in Port of Nuku'alofa confirms a similar narrative. Figure 6.7 shows a stable average count of vessels from 2020 to 2021, with a marked spike in the first quarter of 2022 coinciding with the volcanic eruption. Further investigation of more granular data supports the attribution of increased ship counts to the arrival of rescue-related vessels.

Other insights emerge when daily ship counts are disaggregated by vessel category. Figure 6.8a shows a notable decline in the number of trade-related ships from April 2019 onward, implying a significant decrease in trade-related maritime activity in that period. Figure 6.8b likewise tells of a steady decline in the number of passenger-related vessels. A deeper investigation of trends for this vessel category reveals that cruise ships were only present in the Port of Nuku'alofa in 2019, and again from October 2022 onward. No cruise ships were present in 2020 and 2021. Both RORO vessels and passenger ships were present in the port from 2019 to 2022, albeit in small numbers of less than five. The number of naval vessels, meanwhile, spiked immediately after the volcanic eruption in January 2022, likely due to response and relief efforts (Figure 6.8c).

Overall, these findings make a strong case for the usefulness of AIS data to generate

Figure 6.6: Monthly Heatmap of Automatic Identification System Locations, Port of Nuku'alofa, December 2021–April 2022

Sources: Asian Development Bank calculations using United Nations Global Platform for Official Statistics. 2023. AIS Data. https://officialstatistics.org/ (accessed 31 August 2023); Maps are generated using V. Agafonkin, et al. 2023. Leaflet / Leaflet v.1.9.4. https://leafletjs.com/; OpenStreetMap. https://www.openstreetmap.org/copyright.; and Carto. https://carto.com/attribution/.

Click here for figure data.

Figure 6.7: Daily Count of Unique Vessels, Port of Nuku'alofa, 2019–2023

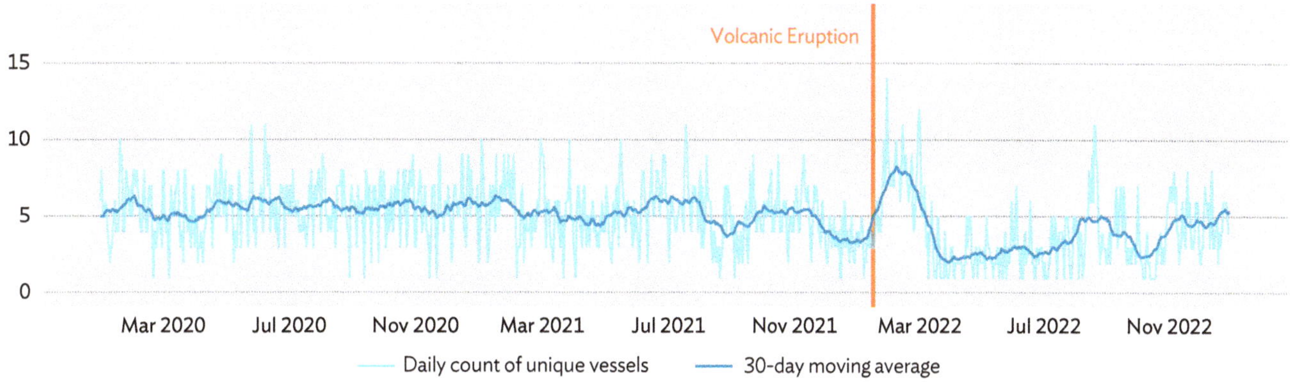

Notes:
1. Figure excludes dates affected by data quality issues (12 May 2022; 14 February 2023).
2. Volcanic eruption: 15 January 2022.
Source: Asian Development Bank calculations using United Nations Global Platform for Official Statistics. 2023. AIS Data. https://officialstatistics.org/ (accessed 31 August 2023).

Click here for figure data.

Figure 6.8: Daily Count of Unique Vessels by Category, Port of Nuku'alofa, 2019–2023

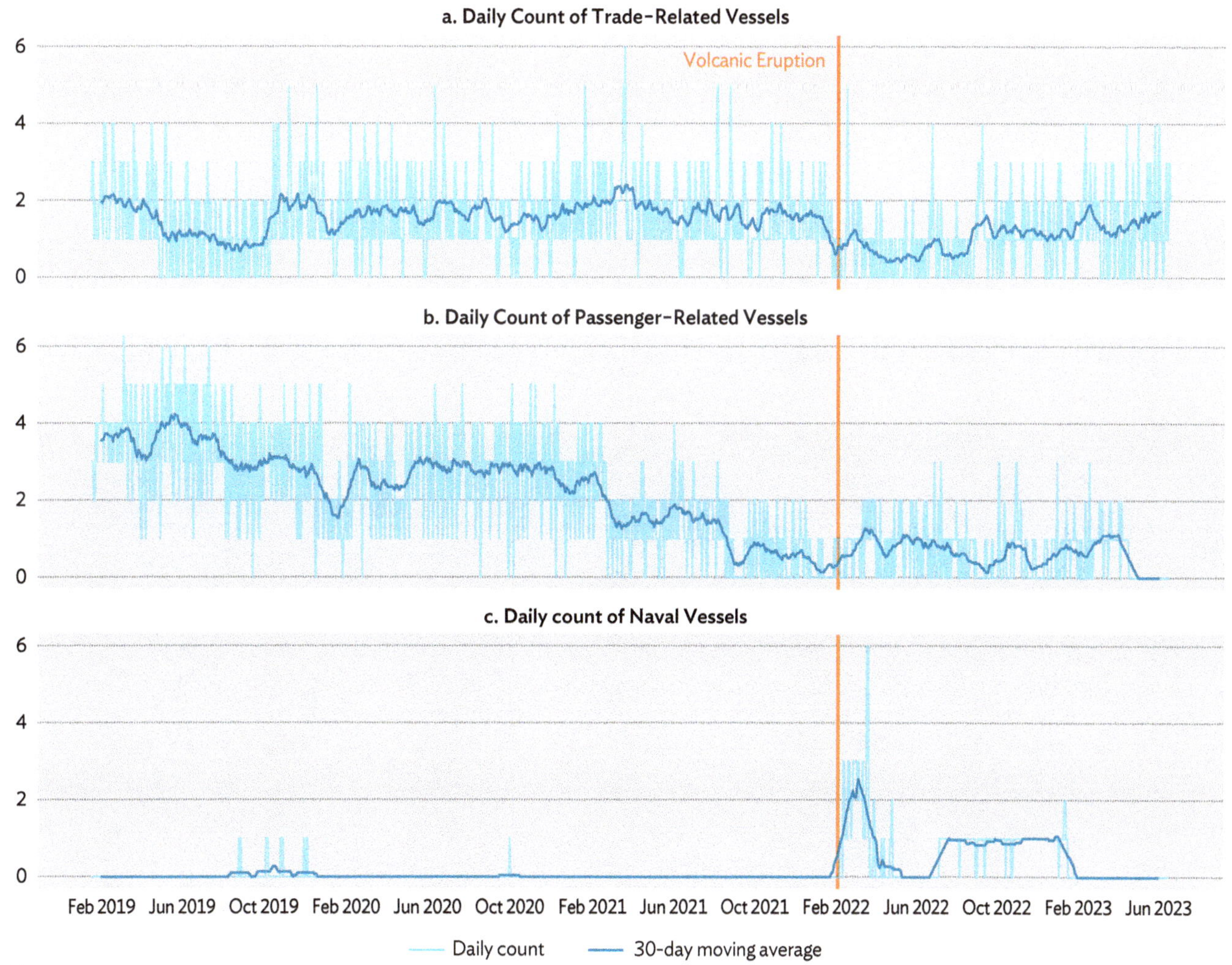

Notes:
1. Figure excludes dates affected by data quality issues (12 May 2022; 14 February 2023). Trade-related vessels consist of cargo and tanker categories (see Table 3.1).
2. Volcanic eruption: 15 January 2022.
Source: Asian Development Bank calculations using United Nations Global Platform for Official Statistics. 2023. AIS Data and Ship Registry Dataset. https://officialstatistics.org/ (accessed 31 August 2023).

Click here for figure data.

reliable indicators of maritime activity. It should be noted however that for small economies, the counts derived are small. Still, AIS provides a way for small economies, where compiling statistics through traditional methods such as surveys can be challenging, to generate reliable economic indicators. For the Port of Nuku'alofa, AIS data accurately reflected a spike in the number of ships from January to February 2022, including naval and rescue ships providing relief following the volcanic eruption of Hunga Tonga–Hunga Ha'apai in Tonga. Likewise, for the Port of Odesa in Ukraine, the substantial decline in ship counts from March 2022 corresponded with the impact of the Russian invasion. Indicators generated for the Bosphorus and Dardanelles straits—Turkish straits leading to the Black Sea—also exhibited a steep decline in vessel transits in February 2022, signifying the impact of the Russian invasion of Ukraine.

Chapter 7

Summary and Conclusion

The compilation and publication of official statistics can take months, indeed years, thereby compromising the effectiveness of the indicators, analyses and policies based on them. Recent technological innovations have enabled the exploration of big data to identify alternative indicators that could potentially signal economic activity, including disruptions to the economy. Among these are data culled from the Automatic Identification System (AIS), which was originally developed to prevent vessel collisions but is gaining prominence as a data source for research and analytical purposes.

Earlier research applications of AIS include analyses to assess port performance, estimate trade flows, and monitor fisheries and maritime carbon dioxide emissions. This study explores the use of AIS data as a potential alternative source for more timely economic statistics compared to official trade data, which are usually published with a lag of a few to several months. AIS shows strong potential as an alternative data source for compiling more timely statistics. AIS messages transmitted by vessels contain data of high volume, velocity, and variety—attributes that allow AIS to offer several benefits over traditional data sources used in official statistics. For example, since AIS data is available in real time, it could serve as an alternative source of maritime statistics, even trade indicators, until official numbers become available. In fact, the statistical offices of the United Kingdom, Ireland, and Denmark use AIS to fill the time gap between data collection and release for certain indicators.

Given the promise shown by AIS data, this report aimed to develop a framework to derive indicators that leverage its usefulness for unlocking maritime insights. The framework introduced Events of Interest (EOIs) and Areas of Interest (AOIs) as the fundamental components of these AIS-derived indicators. The methods employed here address common challenges in using AIS data such as data quality, big data processing, and identification of geographical boundaries.

To assess the effectiveness of AIS-derived indicators in capturing changes in port activity, the DBSCAN algorithm was used to delineate boundaries for key ports such as the combined ports of Los Angeles and Long Beach in the US, the Port of Rotterdam in the Netherlands, and the Port of Shanghai in the PRC. The analysis reveals that these indicators accurately reflected significant events affecting these ports, including congestion in the ports of Los Angeles and Long Beach throughout 2021 and the lockdown measures implemented in Shanghai from March to May 2022. Results reveal that AIS-derived indicators resemble official data, underscoring the potential of AIS as an alternative data source for maritime statistics. AIS-derived transit statistics for the Suez Canal and Panama Canal were almost identical to official figures, while AIS-derived port statistics for the ports of Los Angeles and Long Beach followed the trend from official data.

AIS-derived indicators for select maritime hubs also reflect the impact of globally significant events on maritime activities. The indicators captured the effects of stringent lockdowns due to COVID-19, which drove down maritime activity from passenger vessels while cargo vessels and tankers remained steady. By February 2022, maritime activity saw an uptick, with a return to baseline levels particularly for tankers and passenger vessels, coinciding with the recovery from the pandemic and, interestingly, the Russian invasion of Ukraine. Regional indicators also suggest stability in maritime activity amid successive lockdowns and high oil price volatility.

The report also examined traffic along key maritime passageways. When validated, the counts derived using proposed methods showed that AIS indicators for the Suez Canal captured the disruption caused by the blockage of the Ever Given in March 2021. This is apparent in a significant drop in vessel transits through the canal and a notable increase in median transit times.

Further, to determine if AIS data can be used to generate high-frequency and timely indicators for disruptions to maritime and trade activity, the report focused on recent disruptions to major ports caused by war (Port of Odesa in Ukraine), economic crisis (Port of Colombo in Sri Lanka), and disasters (Port of Nuku'alofa in Tonga). The indicators generated cover various aspects of port activity, such as the count of ships within specific AOIs, the number of ship arrivals, and the duration of time spent in port. In addition, the count of unique vessels indicator was further investigated according to three ship categories: trade-related vessels (encompassing cargo and tanker categories), passenger-related vessels (consisting of roll-on/roll-off passenger; passenger; and cruise ships), and naval ships.

The report's findings make a strong case for the usefulness of AIS data to generate reliable indicators of maritime activity. For the Port of Nuku'alofa, AIS data accurately reflected a spike in the number of ships from January to February 2022, including naval and rescue ships providing relief following the volcanic eruption of Hunga Tonga–Hunga Ha'apai in Tonga. Likewise, for the Port of Odesa in Ukraine, the substantial decline in ship counts from March 2022 corresponded with the impact of the Russian invasion. Indicators generated for the Bosphorus and Dardanelles straits—Turkish straits leading to the Black Sea—also exhibited a steep decline in vessel transits in February 2022, signifying the impact of the Russian invasion of Ukraine.

Overall, these results highlight the potential of AIS-derived indicators as a real-time alternative to official maritime statistics, providing valuable insights long before their official release. This report helped to identify shortcomings posed by AIS data, such as potential signal gaps from transponders being turned off, variations in sampling methods, errors in manually input fields, incorrect MMSIs or ship identifiers, and the possibility of spoofing or manipulation. These indicators were not developed to replace official maritime statistics, but rather to provide high-frequency, near real-time insights on maritime activity and global supply chain dynamics, as a supplement prior to the release of official statistics. The report has further shown how compiling indicators at the early stages of events or disruptions could offer valuable insights that might help policymakers mitigate their adverse effects.

AIS demonstrates strong potential as a supplementary data source for official statistics. While not without data quality issues, its high frequency, volume, and variety of information offers many benefits for policymaking and research over traditional data sources. However, it is crucial to note that while AIS data provides a readily available data source for analyzing global shipping activities, additional information—such as trade statistics, economic indicators, and port-specific data—are needed to provide exhaustive context to the economic implications of the observed trends in global shipping activities. In its current form, AIS data must be used in conjunction with other data sources to ensure accuracy and completeness.

Appendix

Global Movements Data

In this report, the framework for deriving indicators using Automatic Identification System (AIS) data is built around identifying Events of Interest (EOIs) and Areas of Interest (AOIs). Signals referring to EOIs can generally be determined by checking the vessel's speed and location when the signal was sent. A vessel that is stationary within a port boundary implies port activity, while a vessel moving within a passageway boundary implies a transit. While these alone are insufficient to identify 'true' EOIs, they help users distinguish important pieces of information in AIS data. This concept forms the foundation for the vessel movement aggregation method used in the report. Presenting AIS data in terms of vessel movements significantly reduces the volume of data while retaining important information on a vessel's movements. Applying this method to all AIS data points produces the Global Movements Data, which provides a means to efficiently generate indicators with wider coverage as opposed to using UNGP-AIS directly.

Movement Aggregation Method

A vessel movement is defined as the set of consecutive signals that determine if a vessel is stationary, and if it is in an AOI. The method assumes that the information at the start and end of movements are most important, while other movements in between can be aggregated. Four types of movements are possible: (i) stationary in an AOI, (ii) stationary outside an AOI, (iii) not stationary in an AOI, and (iv) not stationary outside an AOI. For each vessel, consecutive AIS messages that belong to a single movement are grouped together. The resulting movement will have information from the first and last AIS messages; and summary statistics (i.e., minimum, maximum, and average), as applicable, from all AIS messages.

To illustrate, consider vessel MV XYZ which is traveling from port A to port B to unload cargo. One-way travel takes a single day, and at port B, loading and unloading takes 12 hours. The frequency of sending AIS messages mainly depends on whether the ship is stationary or not. Assuming the vessel sends position reports every 10 seconds when moving and every 6 minutes when stationary, and that the ship only stopped when it reached the berth to unload, one can estimate the total number of messages sent as 8,640 per way and 120 during the port visit—amounting to 17,400 messages. These 17,400 messages can then be grouped into movements according to their sequence of occurrence:

1. **Not stationary, outside AOI** - Messages sent as ship moved from Port A boundary to Port B boundary, estimated to be around 8,600 messages.

2. **Not stationary, within AOI** - Messages sent as ship moved from Port B boundary to the berth and right before it stopped (this number is expected to be small because traveling from the port boundary to the berth would not take long).

3. **Stationary, within AOI** - Messages sent from the stop while in the berth, estimated to be around 120 messages.

4. **Not stationary, within AOI -** Messages sent while moving from the berth to Port B boundary (similar to point 2, the number of messages should be small).

5. **Not stationary, outside AOI** - Messages sent while moving from Port B boundary to Port A boundary, estimated to be around 8,600 messages.

The first and last AIS messages and any other summary statistics needed are then computed for each movement. To illustrate further, the timestamps of the first AIS message in movement 2 above marks the arrival of the ship in port B. The timestamps of the last AIS message in movement 4 marks the departure from Port B. The difference between these two time stamps is the time spent in Port B.

Movement 3 is the sole EOI among all the movements, since it is the only time the ship stopped. The difference between the first and last time stamps for movement 3 can also be used to calculate the time taken to unload cargo. Further, the first and last draught values for movement 3 might be used to glean the change in draught after the cargo was unloaded, assuming draught values are consistently updated by the vessel crew.

Global Movements data

To generate the Global Movements Data, the Movement Aggregation Method was applied to all AIS data in UNGP-AIS. The distance-based approach was used to generate AOIs for all ports in the world based on the World Port Index database. Each message was assigned a location, according to whether they are within the AOI or not. For cases when the AOIs overlap, the nearest AOI based on the location of the message is assigned. Each message was also flagged whether a vessel is stationary or not. The movement aggregation method was applied monthly to AIS data from January 2019 to May 2023. The resulting data generated approximately 443.1 million movements yearly, a 96% reduction from an annual average of 10.5 billion AIS messages.

Identifying Port Calls/Validation

To test if the Global Movements Data is useful, the dataset was used to replicate actual voyages of major carriers. The schedule of voyages for seven Ever Green carriers (Evergreen Line; Evergreen Marine; Evergreen Marine UK; Evergreen Marine Hong Kong, China; Evergreen Marine Singapore; Evergreen Marine Asia; and Italia Maritima) were extracted from ShipmentLink website from March to April 2023. This was comprised of 5,493 port calls by 714 vessels, covering 245 ports.[1]

1 Only retained port calls from vessels with identifiable IMO number either through Ship Registry data or through third-party providers such as MarineTraffic and VesselFinder were validated. There were 18 vessels excluded from the analysis.

From the Global Movements Data, movements from stationary vessels within AOIs were extracted from March to April 2023 for the 714 vessels. The movements were then aggregated by combining consecutive movements within the same AOI for a single ship. For example, a vessel inside a port waiting to berth will have three movements: (i) the stop while in the waiting area; (ii) the transfer from the waiting area to the berth; and (iii) the stop at the berth. The first and last movements were extracted and aggregated into one movement. Finally, only movements within 3 days of the arrival date of the scheduled voyages were retained. The extra days serve as tolerance for matching the day of arrival.

A total of 5,418 aggregated movements were produced using this process. Each movement was paired with its respective scheduled voyage by matching the IMO, port, and date of arrival. In total, 63% of port calls were matched using the exact day of arrival, and 83% with 3 days tolerance. Figure A.1 visualizes the voyage for sample vessel CMA CGM EVERGLADE using port calls derived from the Global Movements Data and scheduled voyage from ShipmentLink. The figure indicates that the Global Movements Data can retain information on actual vessel port visits.

Figure A.1: Scheduled Voyage and Automatic Identification System-Based Port Calls for Vessel CMA CGM EVERGLADE

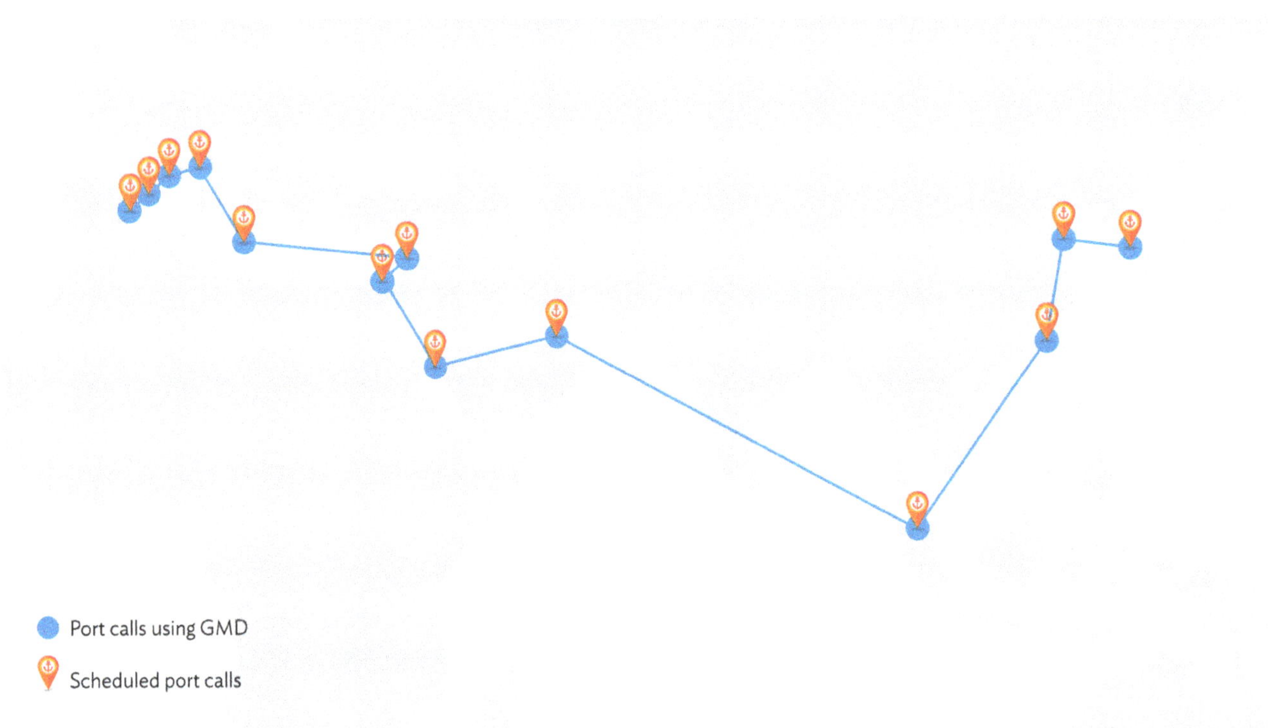

GMD = Global Movements Data.
Sources: Vessel Schedules of CMA CGM EVERGLADE. ShipmentLink https://ss.shipmentlink.com/tvs2/jsp/TVS2_VesselSchedule.jsp?vslCode=CCEG&vslNasme= (accessed 16 June 2023); National Geospatial Intelligence Agency. 2020. World Port Index (Pub 150). https://msi.nga.mil/Publications/WPI; Asian Development Bank calculations using United Nations Global Platform for Official Statistics. 2023. AIS Data. https://officialstatistics.org/ (accessed 31 August 2023); Maps are generated using V. Agafonkin, et al. 2023. Leaflet / Leaflet v.1.9.4. https://leafletjs.com/; OpenStreetMap. https://www.openstreetmap.org/copyright.; and Carto. https://carto.com/attribution/.

Click here for figure data.

References

Allianz Global Corporate & Specialty. 2022. Impact of Ukraine war on global shipping. *Safety and Shipping Review 2022*. https://www.agcs.allianz.com/news-and-insights/expert-risk-articles/shipping-safety-22-ukraine-war.html.

A. Androjna, et al. 2021. AIS Data Vulnerability Indicated by a Spoofing Case-Study. *Applied Sciences*. 11 (11). 5015. https://doi.org/10.3390/app11115015.

S. Arslanalp, R. Koepke, and J. Verschuur. 2021. Tracking Trade from Space: An Application to Pacific Island Countries. *IMF Working Papers*. 2021 (225). p. 40. https://doi.org/10.5089/9781513593531.001.

S. Arslanalp, M. Marini, and P. Tumbarello. 2019. Big Data on Vessel Traffic: Nowcasting Trade Flows in Real time." *IMF Working Paper*. 2019 (275). p. 34. https://doi.org/10.5089/9781513521121.001.

Asian Development Bank. 2022. Harnessing the Potential of Big Data in Post-Pandemic Southeast Asia. Manila. https://dx.doi.org/10.22617/TCS220186.

_____. 2023. *Asian Development Bank Member Fact Sheet - Sri Lanka*. Manila.

_____. 2023. Economic Applicability of the Automatic Identification System Data: Use Cases and the Way Forward. *ADB Briefs Series*. No. 244. http://dx.doi.org/10.22617/BRF230082-2.

bp. 2022. bp Statistical Review of World Energy. 71st.

Central Statistics Office. 2022. Port Visits Using Real-Time Shipping Data. *CSO Frontier Series Output*. 3 October. https://www.cso.ie/en/releasesandpublications/fp/fp-pvrts/portvisitsusingreal-timeshippingdata/.

D. Cerdeiro, A. Komaromi, and Y. Liu. 2020. World Seaborne Trade in Real Time: A Proof of Concept for Building AIS-based Nowcasts from Scratch. *IMF Working Paper*. 2020 (057). p. 44. https://doi.org/10.5089/9781513593531.001.

The Economist. 2022. "The changing American consumer." *Finance & Economics*, 29 May. https://www.economist.com/finance-and-economics/2022/05/29/the-changing-american-consumer (accessed 30 August 2023).

ESRI Data and Maps. 2018. World UTM Grid Dataset. https://hub.arcgis.com/datasets/esri::world-utm-grid/ (accessed 21 June 2023).

M. Ester, et al. 1996. A density-based algorithm for discovering clusters in large spatial databases with noise. *Knowledge Discovery and Data Mining.* 96. pp. 226-231.

G. Fuentes, and R. Adland. 2020. A Spatial Framework for Extracting Suez Canal Transit Information from AIS. *2020 IEEE International Conference on Industrial Engineering and Engineering Management (IEEM).* 14–17 December. https://doi.org/10.1109/IEEM45057.2020.9309882.

I. Heiland, et al. 2019. DP14193 Trade from Space: Shipping Networks and the Global Implications of Local Shocks. *CEPR Discussion Paper.* No. DP14193. https://cepr.org/publications/dp14193.

J. Hoffman, and J. Hoffman. 2020. Ports in the global liner shipping network: Understanding their position, connectivity, and changes over time. *UNCTAD Transport and Trade Facilitation Newsletter.* 10 August. https://unctad.org/news/ports-global-liner-shipping-network-understanding-their-position-connectivity-and-changes-over (accessed 26 June 2023).

Y. Hu, and J. Yao. 2019. Illuminating Economic Growth. *IMF Working Papers.* 2019 (077). p. 57. https://doi.org/10.5089/9781498302944.001.

D. Karnoji, V. Gurudev, and D. Siddaramaiah. 2021. Factors affecting the Vessel Turnaround time in a Seaport. *HYDRO-2020 International Conference.* 26-28 March. https://www.researchgate.net/publication/350654572_Factors_affecting_the_Vessel_Turnaround_time_in_a_Seaport.

W. Komiss, and L. Huntzinger. 2011. The Economic Implications of Disruptions to Maritime Oil Chokepoints. The Center for Naval Analyses. https://www.cna.org/reports/2011/economic-implications-to-disrupting-oil-chokepoints.

D. Laney. 2001. 3D Data Management: Controlling Data Volume, Velocity, and Variety. Application Delivery Strategies by META Group Inc.

R. Meade. 2022. Sri Lanka ports remain insulated from economic collapse for now. *Lloyd's List.* 14 July. https://lloydslist.maritimeintelligence.informa.com/LL1141613/Sri-Lanka-ports-remain-insulated-from-economic-collapse-for-now (accessed 26 June 2023).

P. Menon, and K. Needham. 2022. Planes, ships head for devastated Tonga as aid operation ramps up. *Reuters.* 21 January. https://www.reuters.com/world/tongans-make-contact-with-world-phone-lines-partially-restored-after-tsunami-2022-01-19 (accessed 26 June 2023).

L. Millefiori,et al 2021. COVID-19 impact on global maritime mobility. *Scientific Reports*. 11 (1). https://doi.org/10.1038/s41598-021-97461-7.

B. Mongeluzzo. 2021. LA-LB terminals sound congestion alarm well ahead of peak season. *S&P Journal of Commerce*. 29 July. https://www.joc.com/article/la-lb-terminals-sound-congestion-alarm-well-ahead-peak-season_20210729.html (accessed 30 August 2023).

D. Moulavi, et al. 2014. Density-based clustering validation. *Proceedings of the 2014 SIAM International Conference on Data Mining*. https://doi.org/10.1137/1.9781611973440.96.

T. Notteboom, A. Pallis, and J. Rodrigue. 2022. Port Economics, Management and Policy. New York. https://doi.org/10.4324/9780429318184.

A. Noyvirt et al. 2019. Faster indicators of UK economic activity: more timely and relevant shipping indicators. November 2019. https://datasciencecampus.ons.gov.uk/projects/faster-indicators-of-uk-economic-activity-improving-the-shipping-indicators/ (accessed 26 June 2023).

T. Ough. 2023. Malacca Strait: How one volcano could trigger world chaos. *BBC*. 18 January. https://www.bbc.com/future/article/20230117-malacca-strait-the-sea-lane-that-could-trigger-world-chaos (accessed 30 August 2023).

Pacific Coastal and Marine Center. 2022. In-depth: Surprising tsunamis caused by explosive in Tonga. https://www.usgs.gov/centers/pcmsc/news/depth-surprising-tsunamis-caused-explosive-eruption-tonga (accessed 30 August 2023).

F. Pedregosa, et al. 2011. Scikit-learn: Machine Learning in Python. *Journal of Machine Learning Research*. 12. pp. 2825-2830.

J. Saul, and E. Baptista. 2021. China's souped-up data privacy laws deter researchers. *Reuters*. 17 November. https://www.reuters.com/world/china/off-grid-chinese-data-law-adds-global-shipping-disruption-2021-11-17/ (accessed 30 August 2023).

E. Shubert, et al. 2017. DBSCAN Revisited: Why and How You Should (Still) Use DBSCAN. *ACM Transactions on Database Systems*. 42 (3). 1-21. https://doi.org/10.1145/3068335.

Statistics Denmark. n.d. Port calls in Danish sea ports (experimental statistics). https://www.dst.dk/en/Statistik/dokumentation/documentationofstatistics/port-calls-in-danish-sea-ports--experimental-statistics-.

C. Triebert, et al. 2023. Fake Signals and American Insurance: How a Dark Fleet Moves Russian Oil. *The New York Times*. 30 May. https://www.nytimes.com/interactive/2023/05/30/world/asia/russia-oil-ships-sanctions.html (accessed 30 August 2023).

Uber Technologies. 2023. H3 v3. https://h3geo.org/.

United Nations Conference on Trade and Development. 2022. *Review of Maritime Transport*. New York: United Nations.

United Nations Global Platform for Official Statistics. 2023. AIS Data and Ship Registry Dataset. https://officialstatistics.org/ (accessed August 2023).

J. Verschuur, et al. 2021. Global economic impacts of COVID-19 lockdown measures stand out in high-frequency shipping data. *PLoS ONE*. 16(4). e0248818. https://doi.org/10.1371/journal.pone.0248818.

World Bank. 2022. Tonga Volcanic Eruption and Tsunami: World Bank Disaster Assessment Report Estimates Damages at US$90M. 14 February. https://www.worldbank.org/en/news/press-release/2022/02/14/tonga-volcanic-eruption-and-tsunami-world-bank-disaster-assessment-report-estimates-damages-at-us-90m (accessed 30 August 2023).

www.ingramcontent.com/pod-product-compliance
Lightning Source LLC
Chambersburg PA
CBHW041756220926
51847CB00014B/229
9789292703660